THE ESSENTIAL
KETO SLOW COOKER
COOKBOOK

D1451658

THE ESSENTIAL
KETO SLOW COOKER
COOKBOOK

65 LOW-CARB, HIGH-FAT, NO-FUSS KETOGENIC RECIPES

THE EDITORS OF RODALE BOOKS

RODALE

Copyright © 2019 by Penguin Random House LLC

All rights reserved.
Published in the United States by Rodale Books, an imprint of the
Crown Publishing Group, a division of Penguin Random House LLC,
New York.
crownpublishing.com
rodalebooks.com

RODALE and the Plant colophon are registered trademarks of
Penguin Random House LLC.

Library of Congress Cataloging-in-Publication Data is available

ISBN 978-1-9848-2604-6
Ebook ISBN 978-1-9848-2605-3

Printed in the United States of America

Photographs by Hélène Dujardin
Cover design by Jennifer K. Beal Davis
Cover photograph by Hélène Dujardin

10 9 8 7 6 5 4 3 2 1

First Edition

CONTENTS

1

KETO BASICS AND SLOW COOKER 101

What Is the Ketogenic Diet?

The ketogenic diet is a low-carb, moderate-protein, and high-fat diet. On the keto diet, 60 to 75% of the calories you consume each day should come from fat, 15 to 30% should come from protein, and 5 to 10% should come from carbs.

If you adhere to these guidelines, your body will enter a metabolic state called ketosis, usually after about one to two weeks.

When you are in ketosis, your body has stopped metabolizing glucose (or sugar) for energy, and has switched over to using fat as its energy source. Ketosis has been the default metabolic state through-out most of human history, and there are many health benefits of being in ketosis—including weight loss,

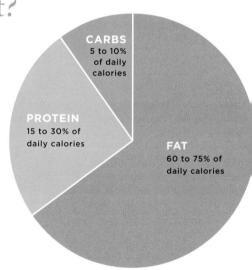

CARBS
5 to 10% of daily calories

PROTEIN
15 to 30% of daily calories

FAT
60 to 75% of daily calories

increased energy, clear skin, joint and muscle pain relief, better sleep, and improved cardiovascular and brain health.

To get into ketosis, you have to limit the amount of glucose the body has available, which means reducing the amount of carbohydrates you eat.

Once your carbohydrate levels are maintained at a low level and you are burning fat instead of carbohydrates for fuel, your body will begin to produce molecules called ketones. Ketones provide energy to the brain and nervous system. You will test the ketone levels in your breath, urine, or blood to determine if you are in ketosis, especially when you are just starting out.

How to Test for Ketones

Urine: This is the most common method of testing your ketone level, as it's quick, affordable, and accurate. Ketone urine-testing strips are readily available at most pharmacies and online.

Blood: With a blood ketone meter, you prick your finger and a machine reads the amount of ketones in your blood. The results are quick and accurate, but more expensive and invasive than other methods.

Breath: Using a device similar to a breathalyzer, you can measure the level of acetone (a ketone by-product) in your breath. This method is easy to administer, but the device tends to be expensive.

Tracking Macros to Stay in Ketosis

The food we eat provides key nutrients our bodies need to perform at an optimal level. These nutrients are divided into three main categories—fats, proteins, and carbohydrates—commonly called macronutrients, or "macros."

It's important to track your macronutrient intake on the keto diet so you can stay in ketosis. If you go outside your target macro zones, your body may start utilizing glucose as energy again, taking you out of ketosis. Keeping your carb intake as low as possible is the best way to ensure you stay in ketosis.

As a rule of thumb, you should eat less than 20 grams of net carbs per day to stay in ketosis, though each body responds differently to carbohydrates; depending on your height, weight, age, activity level, and other factors, you might find you can eat as many as 50 grams of net carbs per day and stay in ketosis. Testing for ketones often and closely tracking your macros in the beginning of your keto journey will help you fine-tune the breakdown of macros that keep you in ketosis.

There are several ways to keep track of your carbs. Some people like to monitor their *total carbohydrates* per day, while others monitor their *net carbs.* To calculate net carbs, subtract the grams of fiber from total grams of carbohydrates. (Fiber is not absorbed by the body and therefore is not calculated in your net carb figure.) Each recipe in this book includes nutritional information to help you keep track of your macros, with calories, fat, net carbs, and protein grams per serving listed at the bottom of the page. We've made it easy so you don't need to do your own net carb calculations.

Thanks to a variety of excellent apps, it's easier than ever to track your daily macros and adjust your diet as needed to reach your goals. Log your food, calculate macros, and keep tabs on your net carb intake on the device of your choice. Here are a few apps we trust:

- **Carb Manager** (carbmanager.com)
- **MyFitnessPal** (myfitnesspal.com)
- **MyMacros+** (getmymacros.com)
- **The Keto Diet App** (ketodietapp.com)

Eating Keto

FOODS TO AVOID	FOODS TO EAT

FOODS TO AVOID

- **Sugar and sugary foods**: White sugar, brown sugar, coconut sugar, maple syrup, honey, soda, fruit juice, smoothies, cake, ice cream, candy, etc.
- **Grains or starches:** Wheat-based products, rice, pasta, cereal, etc.
- **Fruit:** All fruit should be avoided, with the exception of small portions of berries, lemon, and lime.
- **Beans or legumes**: Peas, beans (like kidney, black, cannellini), lentils, and chickpeas.
- **Starchy vegetables:** Potatoes, corn, butternut squash, carrots, parsnips, etc. Any product made from these starchy vegetables should also be avoided.
- **Low-fat or diet products:** These are highly processed and often high in carbs.
- **Some condiments or sauces:** These often contain sugar and unhealthy fat.
- **Processed fats and oils:** Limit your intake of processed vegetable oils like canola oil, vegetable oil, safflower oil, margarine, butter blends, non-olive oil mayonnaise, and hydrogenated cooking oils.
- **Alcohol:** Due to their carb content, many alcoholic beverages can throw you out of ketosis.
- **Sugar-free diet foods:** These are often high in sugar alcohols, which can affect ketone levels in some cases. These foods also tend to be highly processed.
- **Certain nuts:** Cashews, chestnuts, and pistachios are high in carbohydrates.

FOODS TO EAT

- **Healthy fats:** Whole avocados, healthy oils (primarily extra-virgin olive oil, coconut oil, and avocado oil).
- **Beef:** Ground beef, steak, etc., choosing fattier cuts whenever possible.
- **Poultry:** Chicken, duck, quail, pheasant, and other wild game.
- **Pork:** Ground pork, pork loin, tenderloin, chop, and ham.
- **Other meats:** Lamb, turkey, veal.
- **Bacon and sausage:** Only choose products that do not contain sugar.
- **Fish and shellfish:** Salmon, sardines, trout, tuna, mackerel, clams, oyster, lobster, crab, scallops, mussels (wild caught is best).
- **Whole eggs:** Look for free-range or omega-3 whole eggs when possible.
- **Full-fat dairy products:** Whole milk, butter, cottage cheese, ricotta cheese, buttermilk, sour cream, and heavy whipping cream.
- **Cheese:** Unprocessed, high-fat is best.
- **Low-carb, non-starchy vegetables (+ higher-carb vegetables in moderation):** Most green vegetables, tomatoes, onions, peppers, etc.
- **Condiments:** Small amounts of vinegars, fish sauce, soy sauce, mayonnaise, sour cream, etc.
- **Nuts and seeds:** Almonds, walnuts, flax seeds, pumpkin seeds, chia seeds, etc.
- **Coconut:** Coconut milk, coconut cream, coconut flour.
- **Low-carb sweeteners**: Stevia, monk fruit sweetener, erythritol.

Stocking the Keto Kitchen

FATS

Almonds
Almond butter
Almond milk (unsweetened)
Almond oil
Avocado
Avocado oil
Bacon fat
Beef tallow
Blue cheese
Brazil nuts
Butter (look for grass-fed when possible, like Kerrygold)
Buffalo tallow
Buttermilk
Cheese (full-fat like cheddar, Colby, feta, mozzarella, provolone, ricotta, and Swiss)
Chia seeds
Cocoa butter
Coconut
Coconut cream
Coconut milk, unsweetened
Coconut oil
Cream cheese, full-fat (in block form)
Duck fat
Dark chocolate (70 percent or higher, such as Enjoy Life)
Extra-virgin olive oil
Ghee/clarified butter
Greek yogurt (full-fat)
Hazelnut oil
Heavy whipping cream
High oleic sunflower oil
Lard
Macadamia nut oil
Macadamia nuts
Mayonnaise (olive-oil based)
MCT oil (such as SkinnyFat brand)
Mutton tallow
Olives (organic only)
Olive oil
Palm kernel oil
Pecans
Pili nuts
Pistachios
Red palm oil
Schmaltz (chicken fat)
Sour cream (full-fat)
Suet
Sugar-free, stevia-sweetened chocolate (such as Lily's)
Sunflower seeds
Walnuts

PROTEINS

Almond butter
Anchovies
Bacon
Beef (rib eye, porterhouse, T-bone, tenderloin, jerky)
Boar
Buffalo
Catfish
Chicken (breast, leg, thigh, wing, drumstick)
Chicken livers
Clams
Crab
Duck
Eggs (chicken, duck, goose, ostrich, and quail)
Elk
Game hen
Goat
Goose
Greek yogurt (full-fat)
Halibut
Hemp hearts
Herring
Lamb
Lobster
Mackerel
Mahi mahi
Miso
Mussels
Natto
Nut butters (natural, unsweetened)
Nutritional yeast
Oysters
Pork (chops, loin, hocks, tenderloin, ribs)
Pheasant
Prawns
Quail
Rabbit
Salami
Salmon
Sardines
Sausage
Sea bass
Seitan
Scallops
Shrimp
Spirulina
Snapper
Sunflower butter
Swordfish
Tofu
Tempeh
Trout
Tuna (ahi, canned)
Turkey
Walleye
Whitefish (cod, bluegill)
Venison

LOW-CARB VEGETABLES AND FRUITS

Artichokes
Arugula
Asparagus
Avocado
Bok choy
Broccoli
Cabbage
Capers
Cauliflower
Celery
Chard
Coconut
Collard greens
Cucumber
Eggplant
Endive
Fennel
Garlic
Kelp
Kohlrabi
Lettuce (red leaf, Boston, romaine, radicchio)
Mushrooms
Okra
Olives
Onions (yellow, white, red; scallions)
Peppers (green bell, jalapeños, chiles)
Radishes
Rhubarb
Seaweed
Shallots
Spinach
Swiss chard
Tomato
Turnips
Watercress
Zucchini

HIGHER-CARB VEGETABLES AND FRUITS (EAT IN MODERATION)

Butternut squash
Blackberries
Blueberries
Brussels sprouts
Cranberries
Green beans
Jícama
Kale
Leeks
Lemon
Lime
Parsley
Peppers (red bell)
Pumpkin
Raspberries
Rutabaga
Spaghetti squash
Watermelon
Wax beans

HERBS AND SPICES

Allspice
Anise
Annatto
Basil
Bay leaf
Black pepper
Caraway
Cardamom
Cayenne pepper
Celery seed
Chervil
Chili powder
Chives
Cilantro
Cinnamon (ground)
Cloves
Coriander
Cumin
Curry powder (and paste)
Dill
Fenugreek
Galangal
Garlic powder
Ginger
Lemongrass
Licorice
Mace
Marjoram
Mint
Mustard seed
Nutmeg
Oregano
Paprika
Parsley
Peppermint
Rosemary
Saffron
Spearmint
Star anise
Tahini
Tarragon
Thyme (dried)
Turmeric

MISCELLANEOUS PANTRY STAPLES

Almond extract
Baking chocolate
Baking powder
Baking soda
Broth (chicken, beef, vegetable)
Cocoa powder (unsweetened)
Coconut (unsweetened shredded or flakes)
Coconut aminos
Dijon mustard
Fish sauce
Hot sauce
Lemon extract
Pork rinds
Protein powder (unflavored)
Sea salt
Soy sauce
Tahini
Vanilla extract
Vinegar (balsamic, red wine, sherry)

Keto-Compatible Sweeteners

NATURAL SWEETENERS COMPATIBLE WITH KETO DIET	NATURAL SWEETNERS TO AVOID
• Erythritol • Inulin • Monk fruit • Stevia, liquid or powdered without additives • Stevia glycerite (thick liquid stevia) • Swerve natural sweetener • Yacón syrup • Xylitol (in moderation)	• Agave • Aspartame • Brown rice syrup • Brown sugar • Coconut sweetener (like coconut sugar) • Honey • Maltirol • Maple syrup • Saccharine • Sucralose (Splenda)

Getting Started with Your Slow Cooker

When starting a keto diet, you may be overwhelmed by this new way of eating. You've restocked your kitchen with keto-friendly foods and now the time has come to get cooking! If you are unsure about the best way to cook meats, soups, stews, chilis, and other dishes, don't fear. Just dust off the slow cooker and let it get to work for you.

Why is the slow cooker such a great tool for the keto diet? Slow cookers are especially well suited for cooking roasts, chickens, ribs and other meat cuts, soups, stocks, stews, and chilis—dishes that with just a few tweaks can easily be made high-fat, low carb, and oh-so keto-friendly! These cookers braise and tenderize even the toughest cut of meat and simmer a stew or chili to perfection. If you have not cooked a roast, or made your own stocks or stew, it may feel a little intimidating. Plus, meat is often expensive and you don't want to waste your grocery money only to end up with a tasteless, tough roast that no one wants to eat. And who has time to wait by the stove, watching and stirring, when you have other things to do?

The slow cooker makes it easy to create tasty, hearty, foolproof keto meals every day of the week—no muss, no fuss.

The slow cooker sometimes goes by one popular brand and its trademark name, the Crock-Pot, but now there are lots of different brands of slow cookers available. It is typically a stoneware vessel or pot that sits in an electrical base and the heat comes from the sides. The basic temperature settings are Low, High, and often Warm, for serving. Newer units may have programmable settings and some are even Bluetooth compatible, so you can control the exact cooking times wirelessly. There are many different sizes and brands of slow cookers available, but the basic steps to start cooking are the same for all units:

Oil the stoneware. First, put the stoneware in the electrical base. To make cleanup easier, many of the recipes suggest you rub the side walls of the stoneware with oil or butter. The oil has been counted in the nutritional analysis of the recipe. If you wish, you may spray the vessel with nonstick cooking spray and omit rubbing the stoneware with oil or butter, but this may slightly alter the fat content.

Fill the stoneware. Typically, fill the slow cooker about half to three-quarters full. To conform to the printed cooking times, a slow cooker should be filled at least half full. If there is less in your cooker, watch the cooking times and realize it may not need to cook as long.

On the other hand, don't overfill the slow cooker. Typically, fill a slow cooker no more than about three-quarters full.

Set the slow cooker close to an outlet. Also, if you have granite and quartz countertops, always place cooking appliances, including the slow cooker, on a heatproof board to protect the counter.

Cover the slow cooker. Always cook with the cover on. Don't let the lid sit askew, and double-check that the lid is centered and flat. While the slow cooker is on, don't peek or be tempted to stir the contents; you don't need to, and anytime you lift the cover, heat escapes and the cooking time will have to be extended.

Cook in the slow cooker. Set the slow cooker to the Low or High setting. (Or follow the manufacturer's directions for using an automatic or programmed setting.) Do not cook on the Warm setting. When is the food done? Our recipes give an approximate cooking time, but always cook the food until it is fully cooked, done, and tender. (See additional tips on the cooking time, page 18.)

Slow Cooker Sizes

- **Small:** 2 quarts, ideal for sauces and dips
- **Medium:** 3½ to 5 quarts, perfect for side dishes and smaller families
- **Large:** 6 quarts or larger, ideal for meat cuts, larger families, and entertaining

Slow cookers are available in round and oval shapes. Small round ones may be best for a dip, while larger oval ones will more easily accommodate ribs or larger roasts.

If you have a medium or large slow cooker, you can usually adapt any recipe to fit. To use a smaller slow cooker than the one listed in the recipe, begin with about half of the recipe. Or, to use a recipe in your larger slow cooker, you may be able to increase the recipe slightly or select a slightly larger meat cut. For optimum results, fill the slow cooker between half and three-quarters full.

Accent the Flavor

One common question people ask about cooking in a slow cooker is how to ensure best results with this "set it and forget it" style of cooking. If you're not tasting as you go, how can you ensure a perfect finished dish? Here are some pointers to get it right every time.

Searing and browning. Browning meats, onions, or mushrooms in a skillet on the stove before slow cooking adds flavor. Sure, it also makes the finished dish look more appealing, but the caramelization that takes place in the skillet (known as the Maillard reaction) adds a complex, delicious flavor. There was once a time when all slow cooker recipes were written to just place all the food in the slow cooker, and this practice seemed to diminish the flavor. Now, many recipes suggest searing or browning the meat first in oil or butter, then placing it in the slow cooker. If your time is limited, you can omit the browning step, but to achieve the best flavor, sear the meat first. You will find recipes that include the browning step, and some that omit this step, so use the recipes as a guide. If time is short in the morning, you can omit the browning step, or if you want to add depth of flavor, go ahead and brown the meat; it is your choice.

Liquids. Meat can be roasted in the slow cooker without adding liquid. If you have vegetables or want to add flavor, add about ½ cup of broth, stock, water, or tomatoes.

Remember, there will be more liquid at the end of the cooking time than what you started with, as the liquids will not boil away. If you are adapting your own recipe to the slow cooker, use these recipes as a guide and begin with about half the liquid suggested in the original recipe.

Vegetables. Vegetables are wonderful in a slow cooker. Today's slow cookers get much hotter, so many vegetables can be roasted to perfection. In general, place the vegetables in the slow cooker first, then place the meat on top.

Herbs and seasonings. Slow cooking often seems to diminish the flavor of some herbs and seasonings. This is especially true of fresh herbs, so dried herbs are preferred. When using dried herbs, the crumbled leaf herbs will hold the flavor better than ground herbs.

Be sure the dried herbs you use are fresh and that you store them tightly covered, in a cool spot. When in doubt, pick up a new bottle, as dried herbs that have been stored too long may lose their flavor or even develop an off or stale flavor.

Fresh herbs are best added at the end of cooking.

Some recipes in this book list minced fresh garlic and others suggest using dried minced garlic. After you have prepared a few recipes, you will know which flavor you prefer. For recipes with a longer cooking time, dried minced (granulated) garlic may provide a stronger garlic flavor in the finished dish. The choice is yours, and you may use either type. Garlic powder is fine for a dip or in a recipe with a shorter cooking time.

Taste and adjust the seasoning. Taste just before serving and stir in minced fresh herbs or salt and pepper to taste before you plate your dish. Other times, a squeeze of fresh lemon or a dash of hot sauce will brighten the flavor.

Expert Tips

Adding moisture to dry meat. It probably seems odd that meat that is falling off the bone or sitting in liquid can taste dry, but it can. This often means the meat is overcooked. Next time, reduce the cooking time a little and see if the flavor and texture improve. Also, be sure to always select the cut of meat listed in the recipe. Today's meat has often been bred to be lean, and on the keto diet we are looking for fattier cuts. When in doubt, ask the butcher at the meat counter for advice.

Preparing meat. The cooking times suggested for browning the meat or poultry or cooking the bacon are estimates and will vary with the initial temperature of the meat, the exact cut and thickness of the meat, the material the skillet is made of, the temperature setting, and other variables. Pat the meat dry before placing it in the skillet. For the richest flavor, cook the meat until it is well browned. Do not turn the meat often; instead, cook it on the first side until it is well browned before turning it. The cooking times for the bacon are also estimates and will vary with the thickness of the slice, the skillet, the heat setting, and other factors. Watch the bacon closely and turn as needed.

Anytime you cook meat, whether in the oven or in the slow cooker, let the cooked meat stand for about 10 minutes before slicing. This will allow the juices to redistribute, which makes the meat taste juicier. Lift the meat out of the cooker and place on a platter. Cover and allow to stand 10 minutes, then slice or carve the meat.

Thickening the juices. The broth and juices that collect in the slow cooker at the end of the cooking time are flavorful. Spoon the liquid over the meat as you serve it. If you want to thicken the liquid, there are several ways to do this. First, cook the recipe as directed in the recipe, then choose one of these ways to thicken the liquids:

- Boil: After cooking the meat or dish as directed in the recipe, uncover the slow cooker, turn it to High, and cook for 15 to 30 minutes. The liquids will boil and reduce, concentrating the flavor. In a hurry? Ladle the hot drippings or liquid into a saucepan and boil, uncovered, over medium-high heat for 5 to 10 minutes or until reduced.
- Add sour cream, heavy cream, or butter: Whisk these rich and flavorful dairy products into the hot liquid after cooking to create a creamy sauce.
- Stir in arrowroot: Remove about ½ cup of the hot liquid from the slow cooker and whisk in 2 tablespoons of arrowroot powder. Return the arrowroot mixture to the slow cooker and whisk. Cover and cook on High for 10 to 15 minutes to allow the mixture to thicken.

Serving from your slow cooker: This is ideal, especially for casual parties when serving brisket, pulled pork, dips, chilis, and so many other favorites. Keep the slow cooker covered and set the cooker to Warm (if available on your cooker) or Low. Serve for no more than 2 hours for optimum food safety.

While you are away: Slow cookers are designed to cook while you are away or busy with other tasks. This makes them convenient to use while you are working, running errands, or just living your busy life. A larger roast, soup, stew, or chili is better suited for those days when you anticipate being away for a while, as their cooking time is longer. Keep the chicken dishes, pork chops, or eggs—which require a shorter cooking time—for a day off or when your time is more flexible.

Reheating leftovers. A slow cooker is not recommended for reheating foods, as food may stay in a bacterial danger zone for too long, plus the food tends to dry out and will taste overcooked by the time it is hot. Instead, heat the food quickly and thoroughly on the stove, in the oven, or in a microwave oven until it is steaming hot throughout. Stir or rearrange the food midway through reheating to be sure it heats evenly. You can then place the hot foods in the slow cooker for serving, if desired.

Make ahead. Many steps for slow cooker recipes can be done in advance. In fact, some dishes can be completely assembled the night before, placed in the stoneware, and refrigerated. The next morning, just place the filled stoneware in the slow cooker base, turn it on, and off you go. This will make your mornings much less stressful. Roasts should be browned just before cooking in the slow cooker. If mornings are a rush, or if you wish to assemble the recipe the night before, this is the time to skip the browning step. Just place the cold, uncooked meat or roast in the stoneware with the other ingredients the night before, and refrigerate it. It will be ready to be placed in the base in the morning. The chilled food and stoneware will slow the cooking a little, so use the maximum cooking time listed in the recipe.

Sudden temperature changes and frozen meat. The stoneware can crack if you expose it to sudden temperature changes, so follow these instructions for cooking frozen foods.

Avoid pouring cold water into a hot crock. Do not preheat the slow cooker before filling.

You can cook frozen meat in a slow cooker. Be sure to add at least 1 cup of warm liquid to the slow cooker to avoid damaging the stoneware. Increase the cooking time by several hours, checking that the meat is done and tender when you serve it. Using frozen chicken pieces is one trick to make a chicken dish cook a little longer, if that makes the cooking time more convenient for your busy day.

Some recipes may suggest you add frozen vegetables or shrimp to a recipe later in the cooking period, and this is fine. Just turn the slow cooker to High and cook these frozen foods until they are done.

Using dairy. Fresh dairy milk, yogurt, sour cream, and cheese are often used in recipes with shorter cooking times or are added toward the end of cooking. Extended cooking times may cause the dairy products to curdle or break down.

Cooking with wine or alcohol. A few of the recipes in this collection list wine in the ingredient list, to be added for flavor. Since the slow cooker is covered, the alcohol will not boil away. The alcohol is a small amount; however, if you wish to avoid alcohol, substitute an equal amount of broth or water. If you wish to boil away the alcohol, at the end of the cooking period just uncover the slow cooker, turn to High, and cook for about 15 minutes.

Cooking Times—A General Guide to Slow Cooking

One of the benefits of slow cooking is that the cook time is not so critical. An extra few minutes won't hurt, so don't panic if someone is a few minutes late coming to dinner or traffic was heavier than usual. But how do you estimate the cooking time when the recipes list such a wide range?

Each brand and type of slow cooker is unique, and the exact cooking time will be affected by the type of cooker and aspects such as the size of the meat, the starting temperature, and electrical voltage. After you use your slow cooker a time or two, you will be able to easily anticipate the cooking time and know if you prefer the food cooked in the minimum or the maximum time listed.

Check the cooking progress after the estimated cooking time listed in the recipe. Always cook until the meat and vegetables are done, really tender, and cut easily with a fork. If not done and tender, quickly cover the slow cooker and let it keep cooking.

When electric slow cookers were first introduced in the 1970s, they cooked very slowly, so meat cuts could cook on Low for 8 to 10 hours or more and not seem dried or overcooked. Today's slow cookers are often much hotter and you will note cooking times, even on the Low setting, of 4 to 6 hours. Once you use your slow cooker a time or two, you will have a feel as to whether your particular unit is hotter. Most people own newer, or hotter slow cookers, so the recipes have been developed for them. If you happen to have one of the older slow cookers, you will need to extend the cooking times.

If you are adapting a recipe to your slow cooker or trying a new recipe, here are some general guidelines for the cooking times.

- **Dips, sauces.** 30 minutes to 1 hour or until melted and hot on High, then turn to Low or Warm for serving
- **Chicken.** 4 to 6 hours on Low or 2 to 3 hours on High
- **Pork chops or loin cuts.** 4 to 6 hours on Low or 2 to 3 hours on High
- **Beef roasts, pork shoulders.** 7 to 9 hours on Low or 3 to 4 hours on High
- **Soups, stews, and chilis.** 7 to 9 hours on Low or 3 to 4 hours on High

Cooking on Low vs. High

Many slow cookers have both a High and a Low setting. Most meat and vegetable dishes can be cooked on either High or Low, or a combination of the two, and the choice is yours. Most recipes in this book list Low, as that is the most popular and works well on busy days or while you are away.

In general, 1 hour on High equals 2 to 2½ hours on Low. You can select the combination of Low and High that works best for your day. Let's say you have about 5 hours until dinner, but the roast recipe you are using suggests 7 hours on Low. If you use High for 2 hours and then Low for about 3 hours, you will have dinner on the table in 5 hours.

When cooking delicate dishes such as those with eggs, or baking cakes, you must use the temperature setting listed. Exact timing is critical here.

Some slow cookers are equipped with a built-in timer, or you may use an electronically controlled timer or outlet. These work well, but a word of caution comes from the USDA. They recommend never allowing any food to stand at room temperature longer than 2 hours, owing to possible bacteria growth. If you delay the start of the cooking, or you want to keep food warm for serving, never exceed 2 hours. Sadly, if you come home after a long day and discover you forgot to turn on the slow cooker, the only safe option is to toss the food.

While people slow-cook in many other ways, this collection of recipes is specifically designed for an electric stoneware slow cooker. Always follow the manufacturer's recommendations for your slow cooker, and prioritize food safety above all else.

How to Bake in a Slow Cooker

Baking cakes, breads, or cheesecakes in your slow cooker is easy and the results are fantastic. The slow, even heat keeps the baked items moist and flavorful.

You will need to use a large round or oval slow cooker, a rack, and a baking pan.

The rack needs to be about 1 inch high, or you can use an aluminum foil ring. The round racks now readily available are popular for slow cookers and electric pressure cookers. If you prefer to make a foil ring, begin with a sheet of aluminum foil about 14 inches long. Loosely fold the foil lengthwise into thirds, then shape into a ring that fits into the bottom of your slow cooker. The foil ring works just as well as the cooking rack you might purchase for baking cakes. The pros and cons? You must store the rack, but you will use a lot of foil, as you will need to make a new ring each time you bake.

The baking pan must fit into your slow cooker. There are two options. If you have a round or oval slow cooker 5 quarts or larger, you can use a round 7-inch springform pan. These are readily available, but you may have to ask for them at larger or specialty kitchen shops or order them online.

If you have a large oval slow cooker 6 quarts or larger, you can use a standard metal 8½ x 4½-inch loaf pan. Look for an inexpensive pan that does not have large handles.

With either pan, double-check that it fits into your slow cooker before mixing the batter. The pan should sit flat and not be wedged against the stoneware walls.

Line the pan with parchment paper and spray with nonstick cooking spray. Fill the pan with the batter and cover it with aluminum foil. Set the filled pan on the rack in the slow cooker. Bake for the recommended time, generally on High for 2½ to 3½ hours. To test if the cake is done, insert a wooden pick into the center; it is done if the pick comes out clean. A cheesecake should be softly set in the center.

One trick to safely and easily get the hot, baked cake out of the slow cooker is to make a sling from aluminum foil. Take a sheet of foil about 14 to 18 inches long and fold it lengthwise into thirds. Place it over the rack and extend the ends up the sides of the slow cooker. Place the filled pan on the sling over the rack and loosely fold the ends of the foil sling over the cake. Bake as directed. When the cake is done, it is easy to unfold the ends of the sling and use them to help lift the hot pan out of the slow cooker. Use pot holders and always be careful, as the slow cooker, the steam, the pan, and the cake are all very hot.

Helpful Kitchen Tools

One advantage of using a slow cooker is the ease; another is the fact that you don't need a lot of extra tools. Nevertheless, you should have some basic tools on hand for preparing slow cooker recipes.

- Wooden cooking spoon
- Cutting board
- Heatproof board to place the slow cooker on (most countertop manufacturers, including those that install granite and quartz, recommend you place anything hot on a protective surface so you don't damage your counters)
- Pot holders
- Large skillet, to use for searing or browning meat
- Measuring cups (liquid and dry) and measuring spoons
- Sharp knives
- Spatula, for lifting meat out of the slow cooker (be sure it is a heavy-duty one and won't bend under the weight of the roast or chicken)
- Tongs
- Whisk

Specialty items for baking in your slow cooker:

- Baking pan that fits into the slow cooker
- Round rack that fits into the slow cooker
- Wire rack for cooling cakes

CHAPTER

2

BREAKFASTS

Pumpkin Breakfast Bake

Tired of the same ho-hum breakfast? Spice it up a bit with this warm and hearty breakfast bake that will conjure up memories of crisp fall days.

SERVES 6

SLOW COOKER SIZE: MEDIUM

1 tablespoon coconut oil, melted

1 (15-ounce) can pumpkin puree

1 cup heavy whipping cream

1 large egg

1 tablespoon protein powder

½ cup chopped pecans

½ cup chopped walnuts

3 tablespoons sugar-free maple syrup

½ teaspoon ground cinnamon

¼ teaspoon ground nutmeg

1. Rub the sides and bottom of the stoneware with the coconut oil.

2. In a medium bowl, combine the remaining ingredients. Transfer the pumpkin mixture to the slow cooker.

3. Cover and cook on Low for 2 hours. Serve warm.

PER SERVING: 325 CALORIES ★ FAT 31 G (86%) ★ NET CARBS 5 G (6%) ★ PROTEIN 6 G (7%)

Coconut Granola

We all have those mornings when we're short on time, but we know that breakfast is important. Premeasure this granola into half-cup portions and keep them on hand for easy breakfasts on the go. On days when you have time for coffee and more, enjoy a bowl of full-fat yogurt topped with the granola and a few berries.

SERVES

10

SLOW COOKER SIZE: MEDIUM

½ cup coconut oil

1 teaspoon pure vanilla extract

1 teaspoon ground cinnamon

¼ teaspoon salt

¼ cup sugar-free maple syrup

1 cup unsweetened shredded coconut

1 cup slivered almonds

1 cup pecan pieces

½ cup sunflower seeds

½ cup pumpkin seeds

1. Place the coconut oil in the slow cooker. Cover and cook on High for 10 to 15 minutes to melt.

2. Turn the slow cooker to Low. Add the vanilla, cinnamon, salt and maple syrup. Stir well to blend. Add the remaining ingredients and stir well to coat.

3. Cover and cook on Low for 2 hours, stirring every 30 minutes, or until brown and toasted. Spread in a baking pan to cool. Refrigerate or keep in the freezer until ready to enjoy.

PER SERVING: 378 CALORIES ★ FAT 37 G (88%) ★ NET CARBS 4 G (4%) ★ PROTEIN 7 G (7%)

Southwest Egg Casserole

This casserole comes together in a snap if you keep browned sausage in the freezer to pop into the slow cooker. It's a great brunch dish for a crowd, and a nice alternative to the basic egg and sausage breakfast.

SERVES 12

SLOW COOKER SIZE: MEDIUM

Nonstick cooking spray

1 pound breakfast sausage, cooked and drained

½ medium onion, finely diced

½ red bell pepper, finely diced

1 (4-ounce) can whole green chiles, drained and diced

12 large eggs

1 cup heavy whipping cream

½ teaspoon salt

½ teaspoon ground black pepper

1½ cups shredded sharp cheddar cheese

1. Spray the stoneware with the nonstick cooking spray. Place the sausage, onion, bell pepper and green chiles in the stoneware. Stir to combine.

2. In a large bowl, whisk together the eggs, cream, salt, and pepper until blended. Stir in the shredded cheese. Pour the egg mixture over the vegetables in the slow cooker.

3. Cover and cook on Low for 3½ to 4½ hours. Serve warm.

★ TIP: Canned whole green chiles can easily be drained and diced a bit larger than the standard canned diced chiles. The slightly larger pieces are especially nice in this casserole.

PER SERVING: 326 CALORIES ★ FAT 27 G (74%) ★ NET CARBS 2 G (2%) ★ PROTEIN 17 G (21%)

Crustless Quiche

Quiche is extremely versatile—it makes for a great brunch or lunch dish, or even a light dinner. This one has all the flavor of a traditional quiche, but without the carb-heavy crust.

SERVES 6

SLOW COOKER SIZE: MEDIUM

4 tablespoons butter, 2 tablespoons softened

8 ounces white button mushrooms, sliced

8 ounces asparagus, trimmed and cut into 2- to 3-inch pieces

Salt and pepper

8 large eggs

¼ cup heavy whipping cream

4 ounces full-fat cream cheese, cut into small cubes, softened

½ teaspoon dried Italian seasoning

1 cup shredded Swiss cheese

Minced fresh parsley or minced tarragon (optional)

1. Rub the sides and bottom of the stoneware with the 2 tablespoons softened butter; set aside.

2. Melt the remaining 2 tablespoons butter in a medium skillet over medium-high heat. Add the mushrooms and cook, stirring frequently, until the mushrooms release their liquid and it evaporates, about 5 minutes. Stir in the asparagus and cook, stirring frequently, just until the asparagus is crisp and bright green, 2 to 3 minutes. Remove from the heat. Season the vegetables with salt and pepper. Pour the vegetables into the slow cooker.

3. In a large bowl, whisk together the eggs. Add the cream, cream cheese, and Italian seasoning. Whisk until well blended. Stir in ½ cup of the shredded cheese. Whisk to combine and pour over the vegetables.

4. Cover and cook on Low for 1 hour. Stir gently. Cover and cook on Low for 1½ to 2 hours, or until the eggs are softly set.

5. Sprinkle the top with the remaining ½ cup shredded cheese and, if desired, the parsley. Turn the slow cooker off and allow to stand, covered, for 15 minutes.

PER SERVING: 346 CALORIES ★ FAT 29 G (75%) ★ NET CARBS 4 G (5%) ★ PROTEIN 17 G (20%)

Cheesy Bacon and Egg Casserole

You won't miss your usual bacon and egg breakfast once you taste this casserole. Leftovers store well in the refrigerator, making mornings a breeze.

SERVES

6

SLOW COOKER SIZE: MEDIUM

¾ **pound sugar-free bacon**

12 large eggs

¾ **cup heavy whipping cream**

¼ **cup full-fat sour cream**

½ **teaspoon salt**

¼ **teaspoon ground black pepper**

¼ **teaspoon hot sauce**

2 cups shredded sharp cheddar cheese

Minced fresh chives, tarragon, or sliced scallion

1. In a large skillet, over medium-high heat, cook the bacon until crisp, 6 to 10 minutes. Crumble the crisp bacon. Measure out 3 tablespoons of the crumbled bacon and refrigerate it to use as the topping.

2. Pour 2 tablespoons of the bacon drippings into the slow cooker. Brush to coat the sides and bottom of the stoneware.

3. In a large bowl, whisk together the eggs, cream, sour cream, salt, pepper, and hot sauce. Stir in 1 cup of the cheese. Stir in the crumbled bacon. Pour into the slow cooker.

4. Cover and cook on Low for 2 hours. Stir well. Top with the remaining 1 cup cheese and the reserved 3 tablespoons crumbled bacon. Cover and cook on Low for 1½ to 2 hours, or until softly set in the center.

5. Turn the slow cooker off. Garnish the top with the chives. Cover and allow to stand for 15 minutes.

PER SERVING: 653 CALORIES ★ FAT 57 G (79%) ★ NET CARBS 3 G (2%) ★ PROTEIN 30 G (18%)

Shakshouka

In this Middle Eastern dish, you cook your eggs low and slow in a flavorful tomato sauce. After just one bite, this will become a staple of your breakfast repertoire.

SERVES 6

SLOW COOKER SIZE: LARGE

3 tablespoons butter, softened

1 medium onion, finely chopped

1 red bell pepper, finely chopped

4 garlic cloves, minced

1 teaspoon smoked paprika

1 teaspoon ground cumin

1 teaspoon salt

¼ teaspoon ground black pepper

¼ teaspoon red pepper flakes

1 (28-ounce) can crushed tomatoes in puree

⅓ cup heavy whipping cream

6 large eggs

4 ounces whole-milk mozzarella cheese, sliced and cut into 1-inch pieces

3 tablespoons minced fresh flat-leaf (Italian) parsley

1. Rub the sides and bottom of the stoneware with the butter. Place the onion, bell pepper, garlic, paprika, cumin, salt, pepper, and red pepper flakes in the slow cooker. Stir in the tomatoes.

2. Cover and cook on High for 2 to 3 hours, or until hot and bubbly and the vegetables are tender.

3. Stir the cream into the tomato mixture. Crack an egg into a small dish. Use the back of a spoon to make a small well in the hot tomato mixture, then slip the egg into the well. Repeat with the remaining eggs.

4. Cover and cook on Low for 30 minutes or until the eggs are softly set. Top with the mozzarella. Cover and cook on Low for 5 minutes more, or until the cheese is melted. Sprinkle with the parsley and serve.

PER SERVING: 293 CALORIES ★ FAT: 20 G (61%) ★ NET CARBS 11 G (15%) ★ PROTEIN 14 G (19%)

CHAPTER 3

SOUPS, STEWS, AND CHILIS

Chicken Vegetable Soup

Nothing comforts more when you are feeling down or better chases away the chill on a cold night than a bowl of chicken soup. This one won't disappoint.

SERVES 6

SLOW COOKER SIZE: LARGE

1 medium onion, chopped

2 celery stalks, chopped

1 whole chicken, 3½ to 4 pounds

1 teaspoon dried minced garlic

1 teaspoon dried thyme

1 teaspoon salt

½ teaspoon ground black pepper

1 bay leaf

5 cups water

4 tablespoons butter, cut into bits

½ head napa cabbage, thinly sliced

1 head bok choy, thinly sliced

1. Place the onion and celery in the slow cooker. Place the chicken on top of the vegetables. Season with the garlic, thyme, salt, pepper, and bay leaf. Add the water and dot with the butter.

2. Cover and cook on Low for 7 to 9 hours. Carefully remove the chicken and place on a tray. Cut the meat from the bone.

3. Pour the liquid through a strainer and return the liquid to the slow cooker. Discard the cooked vegetables and any bones. Stir in the cabbage and bok choy, then stir in the meat. Cover and cook on High for 30 minutes to 1 hour or until the cabbage is tender.

★ TIP: A zucchini is a great addition to this soup, if you want even more vegetables. Cut 1 small zucchini into ½-inch cubes, and add it to the slow cooker with the cabbage and bok choy.

PER SERVING: 661 CALORIES ★ FAT 47 G (64%) ★ NET CARBS 5 G (3%) ★ PROTEIN 50 G (30%)

Old-Fashioned Beef Stew

This beef stew is hearty and warming, and it pairs perfectly with Cauliflower Mash (page 64).

SERVES 6

5 tablespoons avocado oil

1 medium onion, cut into wedges about ¾ inch thick

2 celery stalks, sliced ¾ inch thick

1 leek, trimmed and sliced ¾ inch thick

2¾ pounds boneless beef stew meat or chuck roast, cut into 1-inch cubes

3 tablespoons tomato paste

1 bay leaf

1 teaspoon dried thyme

1 teaspoon salt

½ teaspoon ground black pepper

⅔ cup beef broth

1½ cups frozen cut green beans

1. Rub the sides and bottom of the stoneware with 1 tablespoon of the oil. Place the onion, celery, and leek in the slow cooker.

2. Heat about 2 tablespoons of the oil in a large skillet over medium-high heat. Add about half of the beef and cook until brown, 4 to 6 minutes. Place the browned meat in the slow cooker. Repeat with the remaining 2 tablespoons oil and the remaining beef.

3. Add the bay leaf, thyme, salt, pepper, and broth. Cover and cook on Low for 6 to 8 hours.

4. Remove and discard the bay leaf. Stir in the green beans. Cover and cook on High for 30 to 60 minutes or until the beans are done.

★ TIP: To avoid storing and trying to use partial cans of tomato paste, look for tubes of tomato paste. They are stocked by the canned tomato products in most supermarkets. Use what you need, then cap and store in the refrigerator for up to about 45 days.

PER SERVING: 616 CALORIES ★ FAT: 47 G (69%) ★ NET CARBS 7 G (4%) ★ PROTEIN 41 G (27%)

Beef Burgundy

The French name for this classic hearty dish is *boeuf bourguignon,* and while it is served all over France, many in the United States associate it with the famous cookbook author Julia Child. Serve this beef burgundy accompanied by Cauliflower Mash (page 64), over zucchini noodles, or with riced cauliflower.

SERVES

6

SLOW COOKER SIZE: LARGE

1 medium onion, sliced

8 slices sugar-free bacon

2½ pounds boneless beef chuck roast, cut into 1-inch cubes

1 cup beef broth

6 tablespoons butter

1 pound white button mushrooms, sliced

2 tablespoons tomato paste

2 garlic cloves, minced

½ teaspoon dried thyme

15 fresh pearl onions, peeled (about 3½ ounces)

½ cup burgundy or other dry red wine

1 teaspoon salt

½ teaspoon freshly ground black pepper

1. Place the onion in the slow cooker.

2. In a large skillet, over medium-high heat, cook the bacon until crisp, 6 to 10 minutes. Set the cooked bacon aside. Add the meat to the skillet, in batches, and cook over medium-high heat until browned, 4 to 6 minutes. Place the browned meat in the slow cooker. Cut the crisp bacon into ½-inch pieces and add to the meat in the slow cooker.

3. Pour the beef broth into the skillet and cook until boiling, scraping up any browned pieces. Pour the liquid into the slow cooker.

4. Melt the butter in the skillet over medium-high heat. Add the mushrooms and cook, stirring frequently, until the mushrooms release their moisture and it evaporates, about 5 minutes. Add the mushrooms to the meat in the slow cooker.

5. Stir in the tomato paste, garlic, thyme, pearl onions, and wine to the slow cooker. Season with the salt and pepper.

6. Cover and cook on Low for 6 to 8 hours.

PER SERVING: 695 CALORIES ★ FAT 54 G (70%) ★ NET CARBS 7 G (4%) ★ PROTEIN 43 G (25%)

Vegetable Beef Cabbage Soup

The vegetables slow-cook together for an unforgettable depth of flavor. This soup freezes well and can be enjoyed at a moment's notice.

SERVES

12

SLOW COOKER SIZE: LARGE

3 tablespoons olive oil

2½ pounds ground beef

2 tablespoons apple cider vinegar

4 cups beef broth

6 slices bacon, cooked until crisp and crumbled

1 medium yellow onion, diced

½ cup fresh green beans, trimmed

½ head cabbage, cored and thinly sliced

1 cup sliced white button mushrooms

2 celery stalks, sliced

1 (28-ounce) can diced tomatoes, not drained

2 garlic cloves, minced

1 teaspoon dried thyme

1 teaspoon salt

½ teaspoon ground black pepper

1. Rub the sides and bottom of the stoneware with 1 tablespoon of the olive oil.

2. Heat the remaining 2 tablespoons olive oil in a large skillet over medium-high heat. Add the ground beef and cook, stirring frequently, until browned, 8 to 10 minutes.

3. Place the browned beef and collected juices in the slow cooker. Add the remaining ingredients to the slow cooker and stir well.

4. Cover and cook on Low for 7 to 9 hours.

PER SERVING: 327 CALORIES ★ FAT 24 G (66%) ★ NET CARBS 4 G (5%) ★ PROTEIN 21 G (26%)

Korean Beef Stew with Kimchi

Beef stew gets a bold twist with this Asian-inspired recipe. Topping the stew with kimchi adds even more flavor.

SERVES
6

SLOW COOKER SIZE: MEDIUM

4 tablespoon coconut oil

2 pounds boneless beef stew meat or beef chuck roast, cut into 1-inch cubes

8 ounces fresh shiitake mushrooms, trimmed and thickly sliced (see Tip)

1 tablespoon dried minced garlic

3 tablespoons finely chopped fresh ginger

2 tablespoons Korean chili sauce

1½ teaspoons Korean chile flakes or chili powder

1 teaspoon salt

½ teaspoon ground black pepper

1 cup beef broth

2 tablespoons sesame oil

2 scallions, green and white parts sliced

1 cup fresh bean sprouts

1 cup kimchi, drained

1 hard-boiled egg, chopped

1. Heat 2 tablespoons of the coconut oil in a large skillet over medium-high heat. Add the beef, in batches as necessary, and cook until browned, 4 to 6 minutes. Place the beef in the slow cooker.

2. Add the remaining 2 tablespoons coconut oil to the skillet. Add the sliced mushrooms and cook, stirring frequently, until the mushrooms release their liquid and the moisture evaporates, about 5 minutes. Transfer the mushrooms to the slow cooker. Stir in the garlic, ginger, chili sauce, chile flakes, salt, and pepper. Pour the broth and 1 tablespoon sesame oil over all.

3. Cover and cook on Low for 6 to 8 hours. Stir in the remaining tablespoon sesame oil.

4. Ladle into serving bowls. Top each with the sliced scallions, bean sprouts, kimchi, and chopped hard-boiled egg.

★ TIP: If desired, substitute 2 (1-ounce) packages dried shiitake mushrooms for the fresh shiitakes. Reconstitute the mushrooms with boiling water, according to package directions, until the mushrooms are tender. Drain and slice the mushrooms, then proceed as recipe directs.

PER SERVING: 444 CALORIES ★ FAT 32 G (65%) ★ NET CARBS 9 G (8%) ★ PROTEIN 33 G (30%)

Texas Chili

You don't have to be from Texas to enjoy a good bowl of red. The slow cooker is the perfect way to make chili. Many a chili contest has been won with this method of slow cooking brisket with the chili ingredients.

SERVES
10

SLOW COOKER SIZE: MEDIUM

2 tablespoons olive oil

2 pounds boneless beef brisket, cut into bite-size cubes (see Tip)

1 medium onion, chopped

6 garlic cloves, minced

1 (28-ounce) can diced tomatoes, not drained

1 (6-ounce) can tomato paste

1 cup beef broth

1 (4-ounce) can chopped green chiles, not drained

4 tablespoons chili powder

2 tablespoons ground cumin

1 teaspoon salt

½ teaspoon ground black pepper

1 teaspoon dried oregano

1 cup full-fat sour cream

1 avocado, peeled, pitted, and sliced

½ cup shredded cheddar cheese

1. Heat the olive oil in large skillet over medium-high heat. Add the brisket to the skillet and brown well on all sides, 4 to 6 minutes. Place the browned meat into the slow cooker. Add the onion, garlic, diced tomatoes, tomato paste, beef broth, chiles, chili powder, cumin, salt, pepper, and oregano to the slow cooker. Stir to combine.

2. Cover and cook on Low for 6 to 8 hours.

3. Ladle into bowls and serve garnished with the sour cream, avocado, and cheddar cheese.

★ TIP: If desired, substitute beef chuck for the brisket.

PER SERVING: 424 CALORIES ★ FAT 32 G (68%) ★ NET CARBS 8 G (7%) ★ PROTEIN 22 G (21%)

White Chicken Salsa Verde Chili

Chicken chili, flavored with green chiles and salsa verde, is a flavorful alternative to the standard beef and tomato chili.

SERVES
6

SLOW COOKER SIZE: MEDIUM

6 tablespoons avocado oil

1 medium onion, chopped

1 green bell pepper, chopped

1 jalapeño pepper, chopped

1 (4-ounce) can whole green chiles, drained and chopped

2½ to 3 pounds boneless, skinless chicken thighs, cubed

1 tablespoon minced garlic

2½ teaspoons ground cumin

2½ teaspoons dried oregano

1 teaspoon salt

¼ teaspoon pepper

½ cup salsa verde (without sugar)

1¼ cups chicken broth

1½ cups full-fat sour cream

2 scallions, chopped

2 cups shredded Monterey Jack or Colby-Jack cheese

1 avocado, peeled, pitted, and chopped

Minced fresh cilantro

1. Rub the sides and bottom of the stoneware with 2 tablespoons of the avocado oil. Place the chopped onion, green pepper, jalapeño, and green chiles in the slow cooker.

2. Heat 2 tablespoons of the oil in a large skillet over medium-high heat. Add half the chicken and brown, stirring to brown evenly, 5 to 7 minutes. Place the chicken in the slow cooker. Repeat with the remaining 2 tablespoons oil and remaining chicken, browning well and placing in the slow cooker. Stir in the garlic, cumin, oregano, salt, pepper, salsa verde, and the broth.

3. Cover and cook on Low for 4 to 6 hours.

4. Ladle the chili into bowls and serve garnished with the sour cream, scallions, cheese, avocado, and cilantro.

PER SERVING: 685 CALORIES ★ FAT 49 G (64%) ★ NET CARBS 11 G (6%) ★ PROTEIN 49 G (29%)

Broccoli and Cauliflower Soup with Bacon

SERVES 6

SLOW COOKER SIZE: MEDIUM

Broccoli and cauliflower provide a nutrient-packed punch in this comforting soup. This recipe provides an ample serving of vitamin C and calcium.

2 (14.5-ounce) cans chicken or vegetable broth

1 medium onion, chopped

3 cups cauliflower florets

3 cups broccoli florets

¼ teaspoon salt

½ teaspoon ground black pepper

1 (8-ounce) package cream cheese, cut into small cubes

2 cups shredded cheddar cheese

6 slices sugar-free bacon, cooked until crisp and crumbled

2 scallions, white and green parts chopped

1. Place the chicken broth, onion, cauliflower, broccoli, salt, and pepper in the slow cooker. Cover and cook on Low for 4 to 5 hours.

2. Use an immersion blender to carefully puree the soup (see Tip). Stir in the cream cheese and cheddar cheese.

3. Cover and cook on High for 30 minutes, stirring halfway through. Ladle into bowls and top with the bacon crumbles and scallions.

★ TIP: You may use a blender instead of an immersion blender, if you prefer. Cool the soup slightly, then pour into the blender, in batches as necessary so not to overfill. Vent the blender cover to allow steam to safely escape and blend until smooth. Pour into a deep bowl. Repeat with the remaining soup. Return all the pureed soup to the slow cooker and proceed as recipe directs.

PER SERVING: 371 CALORIES ★ FAT 30 G (73%) ★ NET CARBS 8 G (9%) ★ PROTEIN 18 G (19%)

Broccoli and Cauliflower
Soup with Bacon

Italian Wedding Soup

This soup is incredibly filling, packed with meatballs, sausage, and nutrient-dense kale. It also freezes quite well, making it an easy meal to defrost on busy weeknights.

SERVES

10

SLOW COOKER SIZE: LARGE

4 tablespoons olive oil

1 pound ground beef

½ pound ground pork

8 garlic cloves, 4 minced and 4 chopped

1 teaspoon dried oregano

⅔ cup grated Parmesan cheese

2 large eggs

1 pound Italian sausage

1 medium onion, diced

10 cups coarsely chopped kale

10 to 12 cups chicken broth

1. Rub the sides and bottom of the stoneware with 1 tablespoon of the olive oil.

2. In a large bowl, combine the beef, pork, minced garlic, oregano, Parmesan, and eggs. Form into 1½-inch meatballs. Heat 2 tablespoons of the oil in a large skillet over medium-high heat. Brown half the meatballs, 4 to 6 minutes. Place the browned meatballs in the slow cooker. Repeat with the remaining tablespoon oil and remaining meatballs.

3. Add the sausage to the hot skillet and cook until browned, stirring frequently, 8 to 10 minutes.

4. Add the browned sausage to the slow cooker. Then add the onion, chopped garlic, kale, and broth to the slow cooker. Cover and cook on Low for 6 to 8 hours.

PER SERVING: 463 CALORIES ★ FAT 36 G (70%) ★ NET CARBS 6 G (5%) ★ PROTEIN 27 G (23%)

New Orleans Gumbo

Gumbo is a staple of Big Easy cuisine, and it's easy to see why. The stew-like dish is packed with flavorful seasonings and vegetables. Pass the hot sauce and "let the good times roll."

SERVES
8

SLOW COOKER SIZE: LARGE

3 tablespoons canola oil

2 pounds boneless, skinless chicken thighs, cut into cubes

1 pound kielbasa sausage, cut into rounds

1 green bell pepper, cored, seeded, and chopped

1 medium onion, chopped

2 celery stalks, thinly sliced

8 garlic cloves, minced

1 (6-ounce) can tomato paste

1 (14.5-ounce) diced tomatoes, not drained

1 tablespoon Cajun seasoning

½ teaspoon dried thyme

½ teaspoon dried oregano

½ teaspoon ground black pepper

2 cups chicken broth

1 pound fresh or frozen thawed shrimp, peeled and deveined

1. Rub the sides and bottom of the stoneware with 1 tablespoon of the canola oil.

2. Heat the remaining 2 tablespoons oil in a large skillet over medium-high heat. Add the chicken and brown well on all sides, 5 to 7 minutes. Place the chicken into the slow cooker.

3. Add all the remaining ingredients except the shrimp to the slow cooker. Cover and cook on Low for 6 to 8 hours.

4. Turn the slow cooker to High and add the shrimp. Cover and cook on High for 30 minutes. Ladle into bowls and serve steaming hot.

PER SERVING: 498 CALORIES ★ FAT 34 G (61%) ★ NET CARBS 9 G (7%) ★ PROTEIN 37 G (30%)

CHAPTER

4

SIDES AND APPETIZERS

Parmesan and Garlic Spaghetti Squash

SERVES
6
SLOW COOKER SIZE: LARGE

You can cook spaghetti squash easily in the slow cooker and serve it as a side dish with your favorite meats or sauces. Or, for a real treat, go ahead and make this delicious, creamy, garlic and Parmesan version.

1 spaghetti squash, about 3 pounds

8 tablespoons butter, cut into 1-tablespoon portions

1 large egg, lightly beaten

¼ cup heavy whipping cream

1 cup shredded Parmesan cheese

3 garlic cloves, finely minced

Salt and pepper

1. Prick the squash several times with the tip of a sharp knife. Place the squash in the slow cooker, not touching the side walls of the slow cooker. Cover and cook on High for 3 to 4 hours, or until the squash is tender.

2. Remove the squash from the slow cooker and set on a board to cool slightly. Place the butter in the slow cooker, cover, and allow it to melt.

3. When the squash is cool enough to handle, cut the squash in half. Scoop out and discard the seeds. Use a fork to scrape the pulp from the squash, making long strands. Drain the squash and return it to the slow cooker. Mix it into the melted butter.

4. In a small bowl, whisk together the egg and the cream. Stir the egg mixture into the squash. Stir in the Parmesan cheese and garlic, and season with salt and pepper. Cover and cook on High for 1½ to 2½ hours, or until softly set.

PER SERVING: 310 CALORIES ★ FAT 25 G (73%) ★ NET CARBS 14 G (18%) ★ PROTEIN 8 G (10%)

Garlic Herb Mushrooms

The aroma of the garlic and herbs slowly cooking will drift through your home and call all to the table. These mushrooms are also a wonderful addition to any buffet table.

SERVES

6

SLOW COOKER SIZE: MEDIUM

24 ounces cremini (baby bella) or white button mushrooms

4 garlic cloves, minced

2 teaspoons dried Italian seasoning

¼ teaspoon red pepper flakes

¾ cup chicken broth

6 tablespoons butter, cut into small cubes

¼ cup heavy whipping cream

2 tablespoons minced fresh flat-leaf (Italian) parsley or oregano

1. Trim the mushrooms and place in the slow cooker. Stir in the garlic, Italian seasoning, red pepper flakes, broth, and butter. Cover and cook on Low for 3 to 4 hours, or until the mushrooms are tender.

2. Stir in the cream. Cook on Low for 15 minutes or until heated. Garnish with the parsley.

PER SERVING: 166 CALORIES ★ FAT 16 G (87%) ★ NET CARBS 4 G (10%) ★ PROTEIN 4 G (10%)

Green Bean Casserole

It's time to update a classic dish with fresh new flavors. Instead of canned vegetables and soup, you'll make this delicious casserole from fresh green beans, cream cheese, and Parmesan.

SERVES 8

SLOW COOKER SIZE: LARGE

4 tablespoons butter, 2 tablespoons softened

½ medium onion, chopped

4 ounces white button mushrooms, sliced

2 pounds fresh green beans, trimmed

1½ teaspoons salt

½ teaspoon ground black pepper

½ teaspoon garlic powder

1 cup chicken broth

1 (8-ounce) package full-fat cream cheese, cut into 1-inch cubes, softened

1 cup shredded Parmesan cheese

½ cup sliced almonds, toasted (see Tip, page 70)

1. Rub the sides and bottom of the stoneware with the 2 tablespoons softened butter.

2. Melt the remaining 2 tablespoons butter in a medium skillet over medium-high heat. Add the onion and cook, stirring frequently, until tender, 3 to 5 minutes. Add the mushrooms and cook until the mushrooms release their liquid and it evaporates, about 5 minutes.

3. Place the green beans in the slow cooker. Pour the onion mixture over the beans. Season with the salt, pepper, and garlic powder. Pour the broth over all.

4. Cover and cook on Low for 7 to 9 hours, or until the green beans are tender. Stir in the cream cheese and the Parmesan cheese. Cover and cook on High for 30 minutes to 1 hour, or until the cheese is melted, stirring every 15 minutes. Garnish with the sliced almonds.

PER SERVING: 266 CALORIES ★ FAT 21 G (71%) ★ NET CARBS 8 G (12%) ★ PROTEIN 10 G (15%)

German Red Cabbage

Red cabbage, seasoned with onion, bacon, and a splash of vinegar, makes a delicious side dish for any meat, but it is especially good with sausage, brats, or pork roast.

SERVES 8

SLOW COOKER SIZE: LARGE

1 (16-ounce) package sugar-free bacon

1 medium onion, chopped

2 garlic cloves, minced

1 head red cabbage, quartered, cored, and thinly sliced

¾ cup chicken broth

½ cup apple cider vinegar

Salt and pepper

1. In a large skillet over medium-high heat, cook the bacon until crisp, 6 to 10 minutes. Set the crisp bacon aside.

2. Add the chopped onion to the drippings in the skillet and cook, stirring frequently, until the onion is tender, 3 to 5 minutes. Stir in the garlic and cook for 30 seconds.

3. Place the sliced cabbage in the slow cooker. Pour the onion mixture over the cabbage. Cut the crisp bacon into bite-sized pieces and add to the cabbage. Add the broth, vinegar, and salt and pepper.

4. Cover and cook on Low for 5 to 7 hours or on High for 2½ to 3½ hours, or until the cabbage is tender.

PER SERVING: 269 CALORIES ★ FAT 23 G (77%) ★ NET CARBS 6 G (9%) ★ PROTEIN 8 G (12%)

Ratatouille

This is a popular dish from Provence, in southern France. It almost always includes eggplant and a variety of vegetables simmered and slow-cooked in olive oil. Many French cooks add whatever vegetables they have on hand to prepare this dish. Ratatouille is perfect served hot or cold.

SLOW COOKER SIZE: LARGE

4 tablespoons olive oil

1 medium onion, diced

1 medium eggplant, unpeeled, coarsely diced

2 medium zucchini, unpeeled, coarsely diced

2 red, yellow, or green bell peppers, cored, seeded, and coarsely diced

4 garlic cloves, minced

1 (28-ounce) can petite diced tomatoes, not drained

1 teaspoon dried thyme

½ teaspoon salt

¼ teaspoon ground black pepper

⅓ cup fresh basil leaves, minced

1. Rub the sides and bottom of the stoneware with 1 tablespoon of the olive oil.

2. Heat the remaining 3 tablespoons olive oil in a large skillet over medium-high heat. Add the onion and cook until tender, stirring frequently, 3 to 5 minutes. Add the eggplant and zucchini, and cook for an additional 3 to 4 minutes. Place the sautéed vegetables in slow cooker. Add the bell peppers, garlic, diced tomatoes, thyme, salt, and pepper. Cover and cook on Low for 4 to 6 hours.

3. Stir in the basil. Serve warm or refrigerate to serve cold.

★ TIP: If you would like some of the liquid to cook off, uncover and cook on High for an additional 30 minutes, then stir in the basil and serve.

PER SERVING: 155 CALORIES ★ FAT 10 G (58%) ★ NET CARBS 10 G (26%) ★ PROTEIN 4 G (10%)

Cauliflower Mash

This creamy mashed cauliflower will remind you of mashed potatoes. Serve it alongside roasts, thick stews, or as a side dish. Earmark this recipe, as you will be making it again and again.

SERVES

6

SLOW COOKER SIZE: MEDIUM

1 cup chicken broth

1 teaspoon dried minced garlic

6 cups cauliflower florets

4 tablespoons butter, softened

½ cup full-fat sour cream

½ teaspoon salt

¼ teaspoon ground black pepper

3 tablespoons minced fresh flat-leaf (Italian) parsley

1. Place the chicken broth and garlic in the slow cooker. Stir to combine. Add the cauliflower florets. Cover and cook on Low for 4 to 5 hours or on High for 2 to 3 hours.

2. Pour into a large mixing bowl. Use an immersion blender or a hand mixer to mash. Stir in the butter, sour cream, salt, and pepper. Taste and adjust seasoning, if necessary. Sprinkle with parsley before serving warm.

PER SERVING: 146 CALORIES ★ FAT 12 G (74%) ★ NET CARBS 5 G (14%) ★ PROTEIN 4 G (11%)

Broccoli and Cauliflower au Gratin

Broccoli and cauliflower are a classic pairing. The bold flavors of the cheese and bacon make this recipe shine.

SERVES 6

SLOW COOKER SIZE: MEDIUM

1 tablespoon olive oil

3 cups cauliflower florets

3 cups broccoli florets

½ cup chopped onion

1 teaspoon dried Italian seasoning

½ teaspoon salt

¼ teaspoon ground black pepper

1 cup heavy whipping cream

2 cups shredded Swiss or Gruyère cheese

4 slices sugar-free bacon, cooked until crisp and crumbled

1. Rub the sides and bottom of the stoneware with the olive oil.

2. Add the cauliflower, broccoli, onion, Italian seasoning, salt, and pepper to the slow cooker and stir to combine. And the cream and 1½ cups of the cheese. Stir to combine. Cover and cook on Low for 5 to 6 hours. Sprinkle with the remaining ½ cup cheese and the bacon. Serve warm.

PER SERVING: 364 CALORIES ★ FAT 30 G (74%) ★ NET CARBS 8 G (9%) ★ PROTEIN 16 G (18%)

Spanish-Style Cauliflower Rice

SERVES 4

SLOW COOKER SIZE: MEDIUM

This recipe is superb when paired with Carnitas (page 98) or your favorite Mexican dish. Don't discount enjoying this for lunch on its own.

3 tablespoons olive oil

5 cups cauliflower florets

½ cup diced onion

2 garlic cloves, minced

½ cup canned tomatoes with green chiles, undrained

1 teaspoon chili powder

1 teaspoon ground cumin

Salt and pepper

¼ cup chopped fresh cilantro

1 cup shredded cheddar cheese

1. Rub the sides and bottom of the stoneware with 1 tablespoon of the olive oil.

2. Place the cauliflower in the work bowl of a food processor and pulse to rice, being careful not to overprocess. Place in the slow cooker.

3. Heat the remaining 2 tablespoons olive oil in a small skillet over medium-high heat. Add the onion and cook until tender, stirring frequently, 3 to 5 minutes. Add the garlic and continue to cook for 30 seconds more. Place in the slow cooker. Add the tomatoes and green chiles, chili powder, cumin, salt, and pepper to the slow cooker.

4. Cover and cook on High for 1 hour. Stir in the cilantro and sprinkle with the cheddar cheese. Cover the slow cooker and let it stand for about 10 minutes to allow the cheese to melt.

PER SERVING: 279 CALORIES ★ FAT 20 G (64%) ★ NET CARBS 11 G (16%) ★ PROTEIN 12 G (17%)

Buffalo Chicken Dip

This popular sports bar appetizer can be prepared at home with no hassles. Fill your slow cooker and enjoy this dip with vegetables such as broccoli or cauliflower. You won't believe it's keto-friendly!

SERVES 10

SLOW COOKER SIZE: SMALL

2 boneless, skinless chicken breasts

1 cup chicken broth

2 (8-ounce) packages full-fat cream cheese, cut into cubes

½ cup hot wing sauce

2 cups shredded cheddar cheese

1 cup full-fat sour cream

½ teaspoon onion powder

1 tablespoon chopped scallion

1. Place the chicken breasts in the slow cooker. Cover with the chicken broth. Cover and cook on Low for 4 hours or on High for 2 hours. Remove the chicken from the slow cooker, and using the tines of two forks, shred the chicken. Discard the broth.

2. Return the chicken to the slow cooker and add the cream cheese, wing sauce, cheddar cheese, sour cream, and onion powder. Cover and cook on High for 1 hour, stirring after 30 minutes. Garnish with the scallions.

PER SERVING: 349 CALORIES ★ FAT 29 G (75%) ★ NET CARBS 3 G (3%) ★ PROTEIN 20 G (23%)

Spinach Artichoke Dip

You don't need to go to a restaurant to enjoy restaurant-style food. This recipe will get rave reviews—you might need to prepare a double batch! Serve the dip with fresh vegetables and enjoy.

SERVES

12

SLOW COOKER SIZE: SMALL

Nonstick cooking spray

3 tablespoons butter

1 medium onion, chopped

2 garlic cloves, minced

1 (10-ounce) package frozen chopped spinach, thawed and well drained

1 (13.75-ounce) can artichoke hearts, drained and chopped

1 (8-ounce) package full-fat cream cheese, cut into small cubes

½ cup mayonnaise

¾ cup shredded Parmesan cheese

2 cups shredded cheddar cheese

½ cup coarsely chopped pecans, toasted (see Tip)

1. Spray the stoneware with nonstick cooking spray.

2. Melt the butter in a medium skillet over medium-high heat. Add the onion and cook until tender, stirring frequently, 3 to 5 minutes. Add the garlic and cook an additional 30 seconds. Transfer the onion mixture to a large bowl.

3. Add the remaining ingredients, except the pecans, to the bowl and stir to blend well. Spoon into the slow cooker. Cover and cook on High for 1 hour, stirring after 30 minutes. Sprinkle with pecans before serving.

> ★ TIP: Toasting nuts intensifies their flavor. To toast nuts, spread them in a single layer on a baking sheet. Bake at 350°F for 5 to 7 minutes or until toasted.

PER SERVING: 300 CALORIES ★ FAT 27 G (81%) ★ NET CARBS 3 G (4%) ★ PROTEIN 9 G (12%)

Vidalia Onion and Bacon Dip

This is a go-to dip for your crudité platter. It also makes a great topping for riced cauliflower.

SERVES

8

SLOW COOKER SIZE: SMALL

Nonstick cooking spray

1 cup mayonnaise

1 cup shredded Swiss cheese

½ cup shredded Parmesan cheese

1 cup finely chopped Vidalia or other sweet onion

8 ounces sugar-free bacon, cooked until crisp

1. Spray the stoneware with nonstick cooking spray.

2. Place all the remaining ingredients in the slow cooker. Cover and cook on High for 1 to 1½ hours, stirring every 30 minutes, or until melted and heated through.

PER SERVING: 393 CALORIES ★ FAT 35 G (80%) ★ NET CARBS 3 G (3%) ★ PROTEIN 15 G (15%)

CHAPTER

5

CHICKEN AND TURKEY

Chicken Lettuce Wraps

You will never need to order takeout with this tasty recipe in your repertoire. This works equally well as a dinner or as an appetizer to take to a party.

SERVES 6

SLOW COOKER SIZE: MEDIUM

4 tablespoons olive oil

2 pounds ground chicken

½ cup finely chopped onion

3 scallions, white and green parts chopped

4 garlic cloves, chopped

1 (8-ounce) can water chestnuts, whole or sliced, drained and diced

1 red bell pepper, cored, seeded, and diced

5 tablespoons soy sauce

1 teaspoon sriracha

2 tablespoons creamy-style peanut butter (100% natural, with no added salt, sugar, or palm oil)

2 tablespoons white wine vinegar

2 teaspoons sesame oil

1 head iceberg lettuce or butter lettuce leaves

1. Rub the sides and bottom of the stoneware with 1 tablespoon of the olive oil.

2. Heat 2 tablespoons of the olive oil in a large skillet over medium-high heat. Add the ground chicken and cook until browned, breaking up the meat as it cooks, 8 to 10 minutes. Place the browned chicken in the slow cooker.

3. Add the remaining tablespoon olive oil to the skillet. Add the onion and scallions and cook, stirring frequently, for 2 to 3 minutes. Add the garlic and cook for 1 minute more. Pour into the slow cooker along with the water chestnuts and diced red pepper.

4. In a small bowl, combine the soy sauce, sriracha, peanut butter, vinegar, and sesame oil. Stir into slow cooker and blend well. Cover and cook on Low for 2 to 3 hours.

5. Spoon the chicken mixture into a serving bowl. To assemble the lettuce wraps, diners can spoon the warm chicken mixture into the center of a lettuce leaf and then fold the lettuce loosely over the chicken.

PER SERVING: 393 CALORIES ★ FAT 26 G (60%) ★ NET CARBS 8 G (8%) ★ PROTEIN 31 G (32%)

Wild Mushroom Chicken Bake

What's not to like about chicken baked with bacon, cheese, and mushrooms? This is a rich, filling dish—and yes, it calls for 12 cloves of garlic! In the slow cooker, they break down and mellow into a pleasant, not-too-strong flavor.

SERVES 6

SLOW COOKER SIZE: LARGE

1 cup dried porcini mushrooms (1-ounce package)

6 slices sugar-free bacon

3 to 4 bone-in chicken leg quarters (about 3½ pounds, leg and thigh pieces)

2 tablespoons butter

12 ounces fresh wild mushrooms, sliced (see Tip)

12 garlic cloves, halved

Salt and pepper

½ cup chicken broth

½ cup full-fat sour cream

1¼ cups shredded Swiss cheese

1. Place the dried mushrooms in a deep bowl. Pour boiling water over to cover, then set aside and allow to reconstitute for 15 minutes.

2. Meanwhile, in a large skillet, over medium-high heat, cook the bacon until crisp, 6 to 10 minutes. Remove the crisp bacon, let cool slightly, and cut into ½-inch pieces. Set aside.

3. Add the chicken to the bacon drippings and cook over medium-high heat until browned, turning to brown evenly, 5 to 7 minutes. Place the chicken in the slow cooker.

4. Add the butter to the bacon drippings in the large skillet and melt over medium-high heat. Add the fresh mushrooms and cook, stirring frequently, until the mushrooms release their moisture and the moisture evaporates, about 5 minutes.

5. Drain the dried mushrooms. Transfer them and the sautéed mushrooms in the slow cooker. Add the bacon and the garlic, and season with salt and pepper. Pour the chicken broth over the chicken.

6. Cover and cook on Low for 4 to 6 hours, or until the chicken is tender. Using a spatula, lift the

PER SERVING: 882 CALORIES ★ FAT 68 G (69%) ★ NET CARBS 7 G (3%) ★ PROTEIN 57 G (26%)

★ TIP: Wild mushrooms will give a slightly richer, more earthy flavor to this dish. While many mushrooms are referred to as wild, they are generally cultivated and readily sold in grocery stores. You might choose porcini, chanterelle, shiitake, maitake, or oyster or a combination of these. Foraging for mushrooms is not recommended. If you prefer, substitute white button mushrooms instead.

chicken pieces out of the slow cooker and arrange on a deep platter. Cover and allow to stand for 10 minutes.

7. Stir the sour cream and 1 cup of the Swiss cheese into the drippings and mushrooms in the slow cooker. Cover and cook on High for 10 minutes, stirring midway through.

8. Spoon the creamy mushroom mixture over the chicken. Garnish with the remaining ¼ cup shredded Swiss cheese.

Chicken in Creamy Bacon Herb Sauce

This is the ideal entrée to serve when entertaining a group. But why wait? Make it tonight.

SERVES
6

SLOW COOKER SIZE: LARGE

6 slices sugar-free bacon

2 shallots, finely chopped

4 ounces white button mushrooms, chopped

Salt and pepper

3 tablespoons minced fresh sage

3 tablespoons minced fresh flat-leaf (Italian) parsley

6 boneless, skinless chicken breasts

½ cup chicken broth

4 ounces full-fat cream cheese, cut into small cubes, softened

⅔ cup heavy whipping cream

⅔ cup shredded Parmesan cheese

1. In a large skillet, over medium-high heat, cook the bacon until crisp, about 6 to 10 minutes. Crumble the crisp bacon, cover, and refrigerate. Measure out and reserve 4 tablespoons of the bacon drippings. Keep the remaining drippings in the skillet.

2. Add the shallots to the hot bacon drippings in the skillet and cook, stirring frequently over medium-high heat, for 3 minutes. Stir in the mushrooms and cook, stirring frequently, until the mushrooms release their liquid and it evaporates, about 5 minutes. Season with salt and pepper. Stir in 1½ tablespoons of the minced sage and 1½ tablespoons of the minced parsley. Remove from the heat and set aside.

3. Pound each chicken breast until thin and even, about ½ inch thick. Lightly brush each breast with some of the reserved bacon drippings. Divide the mushroom-shallot mixture evenly over each breast. Roll up each breast jelly-roll fashion.

4. Brush the bottom and sides of the stoneware with some of the reserved bacon drippings.

PER SERVING: 586 CALORIES ★ FAT 34 G (52%) ★ NET CARBS 3 G (2%) ★ PROTEIN 62 G (42%)

5. Arrange the rolled breasts, seam side down, in the slow cooker. Brush the top of each breast with the remaining bacon drippings. Pour the broth around the chicken.

6. Cover and cook on Low for 4 to 6 hours.

7. Remove the chicken to a serving platter and keep warm. Pour about half the drippings into a deep bowl; set aside. Stir the cream cheese and cream into the drippings in the slow cooker. Cover and cook on High for 15 minutes or until hot and bubbly, whisking the sauce frequently. Stir in the Parmesan cheese and the crumbled bacon. If a thinner sauce is desired, stir in a little of the reserved drippings.

8. Spoon the sauce over the chicken. Garnish with the remaining minced herbs, and serve.

Sunday Chicken

What's better than a roasted chicken for Sunday dinner with the family? Pair it with Cauliflower Mash (page 64).

SERVES 6

SLOW COOKER SIZE: MEDIUM OR LARGE

CHICKEN

1 whole chicken, about 3½ to 4 pounds

4 tablespoons butter, softened

1 teaspoon salt

1 teaspoon dried rosemary, crushed

½ teaspoon dried thyme

½ teaspoon garlic powder

½ teaspoon paprika

½ teaspoon ground black pepper

Zest and juice of 1 lemon

SUNDAY SAUCE

½ cup mayonnaise

¼ cup full-fat sour cream

2 tablespoons whole-grain mustard

1 small scallion, green and white parts finely chopped

1 tablespoon fresh lemon juice

Salt and pepper

1. Pat the chicken dry. Rub the chicken with the butter and place in the slow cooker.

2. In a small bowl, stir together the salt, rosemary, thyme, garlic powder, paprika, pepper, and lemon zest. Rub the seasonings over the chicken. Drizzle with the lemon juice.

3. Cover and cook on Low for 5 to 6 hours, or until tender. Remove the chicken from the slow cooker and allow to stand 10 minutes.

4. Meanwhile, make the sauce: In a medium bowl, mix the mayonnaise, sour cream, mustard, scallion, lemon juice, salt, and pepper. Serve slices of the chicken with dollops of the Sunday Sauce.

PER SERVING: 781 CALORIES ★ FAT 62 G (71%) ★ NET CARBS 2 G (1%) ★ PROTEIN 49 G (25%)

Coq au Vin

Coq au Vin, or chicken in wine, is an old French dish that can be traced all the way back to Julius Caesar. It has withstood the test of time and is as popular today as ever.

SERVES
6

SLOW COOKER SIZE: LARGE

4 thick-cut slices sugar-free bacon

3 to 4 bone-in chicken leg quarters (about 3½ pounds, leg and thigh pieces)

1 medium onion, chopped

2 tablespoons tomato paste

2 teaspoons dried minced garlic

4 tablespoons butter

8 ounces white button or brown mushrooms, sliced

1 cup chicken broth

1 bay leaf

1 teaspoon salt

½ teaspoon ground black pepper

½ teaspoon dried thyme

1 cup dry red wine

Fresh thyme leaves

1. In a large skillet over medium-high heat, cook the bacon until crisp, 6 to 10 minutes. Remove the crisp bacon and let cool slightly. Cut the bacon into ½-inch pieces and set aside.

2. Add the chicken quarters to the skillet with the bacon drippings and cook over medium-high heat until brown, turning to brown evenly, 5 to 7 minutes. Place the onion in the slow cooker and place the browned chicken on top. Spoon the tomato paste and garlic over the chicken. Sprinkle with the crisp bacon.

3. Add the butter to the bacon drippings in the large skillet and melt over medium-high heat. Add the mushrooms and cook, stirring frequently, until they release their moisture and it evaporates, about 5 minutes. Transfer the mushrooms to the slow cooker.

4. Pour the broth into the skillet. Cook, stirring to scrape up any browned bits, for 1 to 2 minutes. Pour the broth over the chicken. Add the bay leaf, salt, pepper, and dried thyme. Pour the wine over all.

5. Cover and cook on Low for 4 to 6 hours. Remove and discard the bay leaf before serving. Garnish with the fresh thyme.

PER SERVING: 745 CALORIES ★ FAT 56 G (68%) ★ NET CARBS 5 G (3%) ★ PROTEIN 49 G (26%)

Chicken Tikka Masala

This sauce has a delicate, full-bodied spice flavor that makes slow cooking the perfect preparation method. The chicken nuggets with the creamy sauce are especially suited to serve with simply prepared cauliflower rice.

SERVES 6

SLOW COOKER SIZE: MEDIUM

3 tablespoon olive oil

2½ pounds boneless, skinless chicken thighs, cut into 1½-inch cubes

½ cup plain full-fat yogurt

1 medium onion, diced

4 garlic cloves, minced

1 tablespoon finely chopped fresh ginger

1 teaspoon ground turmeric

1 teaspoon ground cumin

2 teaspoons garam masala

1 teaspoon paprika

¼ teaspoon cayenne pepper

1 (14.5-ounce) can petite diced tomatoes, drained

¾ cup heavy whipping cream

Minced fresh cilantro

1. Rub the sides and bottom of the stoneware with 1 tablespoon of the olive oil.

2. Place the chicken and the yogurt in the slow cooker and stir well. Heat the remaining 2 tablespoons olive oil in a medium skillet over medium-high heat. Add the onion and cook until tender, stirring frequently, 3 to 5 minutes. Add the garlic, ginger, and spices. Cook for 1 minute. Pour into the slow cooker. Add the tomatoes and stir well. Cover and cook on Low for 4 to 6 hours.

3. Stir in the cream. Cover and cook on High for 10 minutes. Sprinkle with the cilantro just before serving. Serve warm.

PER SERVING: 409 CALORIES ★ FAT 26 G (57%) ★ NET CARBS 6 G (6%) ★ PROTEIN 38 G (37%)

Chicken Marsala

The rich, smoky flavor of the Marsala wine adds a depth of flavor to this recipe that is hard to replicate. If you do not have Marsala on hand, you could use dry sherry or omit the wine and substitute chicken broth with one teaspoon Worcestershire sauce.

SERVES

4

SLOW COOKER SIZE: MEDIUM

1 tablespoon olive oil

1½ pounds boneless, skinless chicken thighs

Salt and pepper

2 cups sliced white button mushrooms

½ cup chicken broth

½ cup Marsala wine

1½ tablespoons arrowroot powder

½ cup heavy whipping cream

1 cup full-fat sour cream

½ cup shredded Parmesan cheese

1. Rub the sides and bottom of the stoneware with the olive oil.

2. Place the chicken in the slow cooker. Season with salt and pepper to taste. Sprinkle the mushrooms over all. Pour the chicken broth and wine over, then cover and cook on Low for 4 to 6 hours.

3. Remove the chicken and mushrooms to a platter. Remove about ½ cup of the liquid from the slow cooker and whisk in the arrowroot. Return the arrowroot mixture to the slow cooker and whisk. Cover and cook on High for about 10 minutes to allow mixture to thicken. Whisk in the cream and sour cream. Place the chicken and mushrooms back in the slow cooker; cover, and cook on High an additional 15 to 20 minutes. Sprinkle with the Parmesan before serving.

PER SERVING: 538 CALORIES ★ FAT 35 G (59%) ★ NET CARBS 11 G (8%) ★ PROTEIN 40 G (30%)

Greek Chicken

This versatile, light chicken dish makes for a great lunch or dinner. It is excellent served with riced cauliflower or zucchini noodles.

SERVES 6

SLOW COOKER SIZE: MEDIUM

3 tablespoons olive oil

2 pounds boneless, skinless chicken thighs

1 red bell pepper, cored, seeded, and cut into thin strips

½ medium onion, thinly sliced

1 teaspoon dried minced garlic

½ teaspoon salt

¼ teaspoon ground black pepper

1 (8-ounce) jar marinated quartered artichoke hearts, drained

⅔ cup pitted kalamata olives

⅔ cup chicken broth

3 tablespoons white wine vinegar

2 tablespoons fresh lemon juice

1 teaspoon dried oregano

1 teaspoon dried thyme

1½ tablespoons arrowroot powder

½ cup crumbled feta cheese

1. Rub the sides and bottom of the stoneware with 1 tablespoon of the olive oil.

2. Heat the remaining 2 tablespoons olive oil in a large skillet over medium-high heat. Add the chicken thighs and brown on both sides, 5 to 7 minutes.

3. Place the red pepper and onion in the slow cooker. Place the browned chicken thighs on top, then sprinkle with the garlic, salt, and pepper. Place the artichoke hearts and olives around the chicken.

4. In a small bowl, combine the broth, vinegar, lemon juice, oregano, and thyme. Pour the broth mixture over the chicken. Cover and cook on Low for 4 to 6 hours.

5. Remove the chicken pieces from the slow cooker and place on a platter with sides. Cover to keep warm. Remove about ½ cup liquid from the slow cooker and whisk in the arrowroot. Return the arrowroot mixture to the slow cooker and whisk. Cover and cook on High for about 10 to 15 minutes to thicken. Spoon the sauce over the chicken. Sprinkle with the feta and serve.

PER SERVING: 492 CALORIES ★ FAT 39 G (71%) ★ NET CARBS 7 G (6%) ★ PROTEIN 27 G (22%)

Chicken Cauliflower Curry

Curry dishes can range from mild to spicy but are always packed with flavor. For this recipe, chicken and cauliflower are nestled in the curry-flavored sauce. Top each serving with almonds, scallions, tomatoes, and cilantro, or set out a variety of toppings and let everyone top their bowl as desired.

SERVES

6

SLOW COOKER SIZE: MEDIUM

6 tablespoons ghee or coconut oil

2 pounds boneless, skinless chicken thighs, cut into 1½-inch cubes

1 medium onion, chopped

3 cups cauliflower florets

2 teaspoons dried minced garlic

1 tablespoon finely chopped fresh ginger

4 teaspoons curry powder

1 teaspoon ground cumin

½ teaspoon ground turmeric

1½ teaspoons salt

½ teaspoon pepper

1 (13.6-ounce) can unsweetened coconut milk

½ cup sliced almonds, toasted (see Tip, page 70)

2 scallions, sliced

1 medium tomato, chopped

2 tablespoons finely chopped fresh cilantro

1. Rub the sides and bottom of the stoneware with 3 tablespoons of the ghee.

2. Heat the remaining 3 tablespoons ghee in a large skillet over medium-high heat. Add the chicken and cook, stirring frequently until browned, 5 to 7 minutes. Transfer the browned chicken to the slow cooker. Add the onion and cauliflower to the slow cooker.

3. Add the garlic, ginger, curry powder, cumin, turmeric, salt, and pepper. Pour the coconut milk over all. Cover and cook on Low for 5 to 7 hours.

4. Ladle into serving bowls. Top each serving with almonds, scallions, tomatoes, and cilantro.

PER SERVING: 627 CALORIES ★ FAT 54 G (77%) ★ NET CARBS 7 G (4%) ★ PROTEIN 30 G (19%)

Simple Herb-Seasoned Turkey Breast

This herb-seasoned turkey breast requires no fussy preparation. The result is a moist, tender entrée that the whole family will love.

SERVES
8

SLOW COOKER SIZE: LARGE

3 tablespoons olive oil

1 boneless turkey breast, about 3 pounds

1 medium onion, cut into wedges

2 celery stalks, cut into large pieces

1 teaspoon dried minced garlic

1 teaspoon dried thyme

1 tablespoon dried sage, crumbled

1 teaspoon salt

½ teaspoon ground black pepper

½ cup water

8 tablespoons butter, melted

1. Rub the sides and bottom of the stoneware with 1 tablespoon of the olive oil.

2. Heat the remaining 2 tablespoons olive oil in a large skillet over medium-high heat. Add the turkey and brown well on all sides, 8 to 12 minutes.

3. Place the onion and celery in the slow cooker. Place the turkey on top. In a small bowl, combine the garlic, thyme, sage, salt, and pepper. Sprinkle the seasonings over the turkey breast.

4. Pour the water around the turkey. Pour the melted butter on top of the seasonings. Cover and cook on Low for 7 to 9 hours.

PER SERVING: 384 CALORIES ★ FAT 27 G (63%) ★ NET CARBS 3 G (3%) ★ PROTEIN 31 G (32%)

CHAPTER

6

PORK AND LAMB

Easy Pork Chops

The tomato–vinegar combination provides a nice zing to this meal. You can substitute hot seasoning sauce for the chili paste.

SERVES

4

SLOW COOKER SIZE: LARGE

3 tablespoons canola oil

4 bone-in pork loin chops, cut 1½ inches thick

1 medium onion, chopped

2 celery stalks, chopped

1 green bell pepper, cored, seeded, and cut into strips

¼ cup chicken broth

1 (6-ounce) can tomato paste

2 garlic cloves, minced

1 tablespoon chili paste

1 tablespoon apple cider vinegar

¼ teaspoon salt

¼ teaspoon ground black pepper

1. Rub the sides and bottom of the stoneware with 1 tablespoon of the canola oil.

2. Heat the remaining 2 tablespoons canola oil in a large skillet over medium-high heat. Brown the pork chops on both sides, 4 to 6 minutes; set aside.

3. Place the onion, celery, and green pepper into the slow cooker. Top with the browned pork chops.

4. In a small bowl, combine the broth, tomato paste, garlic, chili paste, vinegar, salt, and pepper. Pour the broth mixture over the pork chops. Cover and cook on Low for 4 to 6 hours.

PER SERVING: 755 CALORIES ★ FAT 50 G (60%) ★ NET CARBS 11 G (6%) ★ PROTEIN 59 G (31%)

Mustard Glazed Pork Roast

This is an impressive, flavorful dish that makes for a great holiday meal. Be sure to use a keto-friendly stone-ground mustard for the glaze.

SERVES 6

1 medium onion, sliced

1 bulb fennel, trimmed and sliced

4 tablespoons butter, softened

1 boneless pork loin roast (2 to 2½ pounds)

1 teaspoon dried thyme

½ teaspoon salt

½ teaspoon ground black pepper

¼ cup stone-ground mustard

½ cup chicken broth

1 cup full-fat sour cream

Minced fresh thyme

1. Place the onion and fennel in the slow cooker.

2. Rub the butter over all sides of the pork roast, coating it evenly, then place it in the slow cooker. Sprinkle the dried thyme, salt, and pepper over the roast. Spread the top of the roast with the mustard. Pour in the broth.

3. Cover and cook on Low for 4 to 6 hours.

4. Remove the meat from in the slow cooker. Cover the meat to keep warm and set aside.

5. Whisk the sour cream into the drippings. Cover and cook on High for 15 minutes or until hot and bubbly, whisking often. Season, as desired, with additional salt and pepper. Spoon the sauce over the meat. Garnish with the fresh thyme.

★ TIP: Have you ever used fennel? Fennel has three parts: the bulb, celery-like stalks, and feathery leaves. For this recipe, use the bulb. Trim off the stem and root end, and peel away any brown outer layers. Cut the bulb into quarters and trim away the inner core. Thinly slice the remaining bulb for this recipe. The stems can be eaten raw in a salad, and the feathery leaves can be used as a fresh herb or garnish.

PER SERVING: 492 CALORIES ★ FAT 37 G (68%) ★ NET CARBS 4 G (3%) ★ PROTEIN 32 G (26%)

Country Ribs with Sauerkraut

This is a simple dish to pop into the slow cooker before your busy day begins. The sauerkraut adds another dimension of flavor, plus plenty of vitamin C.

SERVES
4

SLOW COOKER SIZE: MEDIUM

1 tablespoon canola oil

1½ pounds country-style pork ribs

Salt and pepper

1 teaspoon caraway seeds

½ cup chicken broth

2 cups sauerkraut, drained of excess liquid

1. Rub the sides and bottom of the stoneware with the canola oil.

2. Place the ribs into the slow cooker and season with salt and pepper. Sprinkle the ribs evenly with caraway seeds. Pour the chicken broth over the ribs and top with the sauerkraut.

3. Cover and cook on Low for 5 to 7 hours.

PER SERVING: 369 CALORIES ★ FAT 24 G (58%) ★ NET CARBS 1 G (1%) ★ PROTEIN 34 G (37%)

Pulled Pork in Lettuce Wraps

This Asian-style pulled pork is a refreshing change from American barbecued pulled pork. The toasted sesame seeds add a nutty flavor.

SERVES

8

SLOW COOKER SIZE: MEDIUM

1 tablespoon canola oil

1 medium onion, chopped

1 red bell pepper, cored, seeded, and diced

1 boneless pork shoulder roast (about 2 pounds)

2 garlic cloves, minced

¼ cup soy sauce

1 teaspoon hot wing sauce

2 tablespoon sugar-free maple syrup

1 tablespoon sesame oil

1 tablespoon sesame seeds, toasted

⅓ cup minced fresh cilantro

Lettuce leaves, such as iceberg or romaine

1. Rub the sides and bottom of the stoneware with the canola oil. Place the onion and red pepper into the stoneware. Place the pork on top.

2. In a small bowl, combine the garlic, soy sauce, wing sauce, maple syrup, sesame oil, and sesame seeds. Stir to combine well. Pour the sauce over the pork.

3. Cover and cook on Low for 6 to 8 hours.

4. Remove the pork from the slow cooker. Using the tines of the fork, shred the meat and return it to the slow cooker. Stir in the cilantro. When you're ready to serve, spoon the pork mixture into a serving bowl. To assemble the lettuce wraps, diners can spoon the warm pork mixture into the center of a lettuce leaf and then fold the lettuce loosely over the pork.

PER SERVING: 280 CALORIES ★ FAT 18 G (58%) ★ NET CARBS 3 G (4%) ★ PROTEIN 23 G (33%)

Carnitas

Carnitas are a traditional Mexican style of shredded pork. In this recipe, we serve the carnitas with sour cream and avocado. Or, make a keto-friendly taco salad by serving the carnitas atop of a bed of greens.

SERVES 8

SLOW COOKER SIZE: MEDIUM

3 tablespoons olive oil

1 boneless pork shoulder roast (about 2 pounds), cut into 2-inch cubes

1 medium onion, chopped

2 cups picante sauce

1 cup chicken broth

1 chipotle chile in adobo sauce, chopped

1 teaspoon dried minced garlic

2 teaspoons ground cumin

½ teaspoon salt

½ cup minced fresh cilantro

1 avocado, peeled, pitted, and sliced

1 cup full-fat sour cream

1. Rub the sides and bottom of the stoneware with 1 tablespoon of the olive oil.

2. Heat the remaining 2 tablespoons olive oil in a large skillet over medium-high heat. Add the pork cubes and brown on all sides, 4 to 6 minutes. Place the browned pork in the slow cooker. Stir in the onion, picante sauce, broth, chile, garlic, cumin, and salt.

3. Cover and cook on Low for 7 to 9 hours.

4. Shred the pork with the tines of two forks. Serve the meat with the sauce, topped with the avocado and sour cream.

★ TIP: Chipotle chiles are smoked jalapeños and are often sold canned in adobo sauce. Use one chile for this recipe, then freeze the remaining for another day. (For real convenience, spread the chipotles on a tray and freeze them until they are firm. Pack the frozen chiles in a freezer bag, seal, label, and freeze. This makes it easy to use just a single frozen chile or two the next time you want to flavor a dish.)

PER SERVING: 373 CALORIES ★ FAT 28 G (68%) ★ NET CARBS 5 G (5%) ★ PROTEIN 23 G (25%)

Spinach-Stuffed Pork Loin

This delicious pork roast is so good you will serve it frequently, especially when entertaining. The slices reveal a striking swirl of cream cheese and brightly colored spinach, making it as beautiful as it is tasty.

SERVES

6

SLOW COOKER SIZE: LARGE

2 tablespoons olive oil

2 shallots, finely chopped

3 garlic cloves, chopped

2½ to 3 cups loosely packed trimmed baby spinach (about 4 ounces)

Salt and coarse ground black pepper

1 boneless pork loin roast (2½ to 3 pounds)

4 ounces full-fat cream cheese, softened

6 slices sugar-free bacon

2 tablespoons butter, melted

1 tablespoon coarse-ground mustard

1. Heat the olive oil in a large skillet over medium-high heat. Add the shallots and cook until tender, stirring frequently, 3 to 5 minutes. Stir in the garlic and cook for 30 seconds more. Stir in the spinach and cook until the spinach wilts and the excess moisture evaporates, 4 to 5 minutes. Season with salt and pepper to taste. Set aside to cool for 5 minutes.

2. Cut the pork loin almost in half lengthwise, not cutting all the way through on one side. Open up the pork (like a book) so it lays flat. Cover with plastic wrap. Pound the meat with the flat side of a meat pounder until it is even and about ¾ inch thick. Season the meat with salt and pepper.

3. Spread the cream cheese evenly over the meat, leaving a 1-inch boarder. Spoon the spinach mixture over the cream cheese. Roll up the meat jelly-roll style, starting at a long side, gently covering the spinach and cheese with the pork.

4. In a small bowl, stir together the butter and mustard. Brush the mustard–butter mixture over the pork, covering completely. Wrap the meat in the bacon. Tie the pork roll with string, then place in the slow cooker, seam side down.

PER SERVING: 650 CALORIES ★ FAT 51 G (71%) ★ NET CARBS 2 G (1%) ★ PROTEIN 43 G (26%)

5. Cover and cook on Low for 4 to 6 hours, or until tender. Remove the meat from the slow cooker and allow to stand for 15 minutes. Remove the string and slice the meat. Serve with some of the drippings spooned over each slice.

Barbecued Ribs

The spices and balsamic vinegar combine to make a classic barbecue flavor for these spare ribs. Quickly broil them at the end of cooking so the edges become brown and crisp.

SLOW COOKER SIZE: LARGE

5 tablespoons avocado oil

1 rack bone-in pork spare ribs (about 4 pounds), cut into serving portions

1 tablespoon smoked paprika (see Tip)

1½ teaspoons garlic powder

1 teaspoon mustard powder

1 teaspoon celery seeds

1 teaspoon salt

1 teaspoon ground black pepper

¼ teaspoon red pepper flakes

¼ teaspoon ground cloves

1 (6-ounce) can tomato paste

3 tablespoons balsamic vinegar

1 tablespoon liquid smoke

½ cup water

1. Brush the sides and bottom of the stoneware with 2 tablespoons of the avocado oil. Rub the ribs with the remaining 3 tablespoons oil.

2. In a small bowl, mix the paprika, garlic powder, mustard powder, celery seeds, salt, pepper, red pepper flakes, and cloves. Rub the seasonings over the ribs, then place the ribs in the slow cooker.

3. In a small bowl, stir together the tomato paste, vinegar, liquid smoke, and water. Pour the tomato paste mixture over the ribs. Cover and cook on Low for 5 to 7 hours.

4. Lift the ribs out of the slow cooker and arrange in a single layer on a broiler pan. Broil about 6 inches from the heat until the edges are crisp and brown, 5 to 7 minutes. Serve the remaining sauce with the ribs.

★ TIP: The typical paprika you might sprinkle on deviled eggs doesn't provide a lot of flavor or heat. While Hungarian paprika is the most spicy variety, this recipe calls for smoked paprika, which has a richer taste and will give the ribs a hint of smoky flavor.

PER SERVING: 734 CALORIES ★ FAT 62 G (76%) ★ NET CARBS 5 G (3%) ★ PROTEIN 36 G (20%)

Lamb Ragout

Lamb shanks are a perfect match for the slow cooker. This dish features flavors of Greece, with kalamata olives, almonds, pine nuts, and feta cheese.

SLOW COOKER SIZE: LARGE

2 tablespoons olive oil

4 pounds lamb shanks

30 to 35 fresh pearl onions, peeled (about 8 ounces)

1 tablespoon dried minced garlic

2 tablespoons tomato paste

2 teaspoons dried rosemary, crushed

Salt and coarsely ground black pepper

½ cup chicken broth

½ cup chopped pitted kalamata olives

4 tablespoons butter

½ cup slivered almonds

¼ cup pine nuts

1 cup crumbled feta cheese

2 tablespoons minced fresh rosemary or flat-leaf (Italian) parsley

1. Heat the olive oil in a large skillet over medium-high heat. Add the lamb and brown well on each side, 4 to 6 minutes. Place the lamb in the slow cooker. Add the pearl onions, garlic, tomato paste, rosemary, salt, pepper, and broth.

2. Cover and cook on Low for 5 to 7 hours, or until the meat is tender.

3. Remove the shanks and place on a board to cool slightly. Cut the meat from the bone and return it to the slow cooker. Stir in the olives. Cover and cook on High for 15 to 30 minutes.

4. In a small skillet over medium heat, melt 2 tablespoons of the butter. Add the almonds and cook, stirring frequently, until golden brown, 2 to 3 minutes. Spoon the almonds into a small bowl. Add the remaining 2 tablespoon butter to the skillet. Add the pine nuts and cook, stirring frequently, until golden brown, 2 to 3 minutes. Transfer the pine nuts to a small bowl.

5. Spoon the lamb into serving bowls. Top each serving with some almonds, pine nuts, the feta cheese, and fresh rosemary.

PER SERVING: 942 CALORIES ★ FAT 71 G (68%) ★ NET CARBS 7 G (3%) ★ PROTEIN 64 G (27%)

CHAPTER

7

BEEF

Tomato Pesto Roast Beef

On days when time is short, this is your go-to mealtime solution. It takes about five minutes to prepare this recipe for the slow cooker. Dinner will be ready by evening, and you will have spent minimal effort to create a delicious meal.

SERVES

6

SLOW COOKER SIZE: MEDIUM

1 tablespoon olive oil

½ cup diced onion

1 boneless beef chuck roast (about 2 pounds)

½ cup basil pesto

1 (14.5-ounce) can Italian-style diced tomatoes, not drained

1. Rub the sides and bottom of the stoneware with the olive oil. Sprinkle the diced onion into the slow cooker. Place the roast on the onion. Spread the pesto over the top of the roast. Pour the tomatoes around the roast.

2. Cover and cook on Low for 6 to 8 hours, or until the meat is tender.

PER SERVING: 522 CALORIES ★ FAT 41 G (71%) ★ NET CARBS 5 G (4%) ★ PROTEIN 31 G (24%)

Balsamic Beef

This recipe comes together in just minutes, making it possible to serve home-cooked roast beef any time you want! The radishes add a great peppery kick to the dish.

SERVES 6

SLOW COOKER SIZE: MEDIUM

4 tablespoons olive oil

1 medium onion, sliced

6 whole radishes, 1 to 1½ inches in diameter, trimmed

1 boneless beef chuck roast (about 2½ pounds)

3 tablespoons balsamic vinegar

1 tablespoon dried Italian seasoning

2 teaspoons dried minced garlic

1 teaspoon salt

1 teaspoon ground black pepper

½ cup beef broth

1. Rub the sides and bottom of the stoneware with 2 tablespoons of the olive oil. Place the onion and radishes in the slow cooker.

2. Rub the beef on all sides with the remaining 2 tablespoons olive oil. Place the meat in the slow cooker on top of the onions and radishes. Brush the top and sides of the roast with the vinegar. Season with the Italian seasoning, garlic, salt, and pepper. Pour the broth over all.

3. Cover and cook on Low for 6 to 8 hours, or until the meat is tender.

PER SERVING: 560 CALORIES ★ FAT 43 G (69%) ★ NET CARBS 3 G (2%) ★ PROTEIN 37 G (26%)

Italian Stuffed Flank Steak

This Italian spin on the classic flank steak comes together in minutes in the slow cooker. Topped with tomato sauce and cheese, it's reminiscent of your favorite Italian dishes but without the carbs.

SERVES

6

SLOW COOKER SIZE: LARGE

1 tablespoon olive oil

2 (1-pound) pieces beef flank steak, pounded to ¼-inch thickness

½ cup basil pesto

½ cup sun-dried tomatoes packed in oil, diced

2 cups shredded mozzarella cheese

½ cup shredded Parmesan cheese

1 cup marinara sauce

1. Rub the sides and bottom of the stoneware with the olive oil.

2. Pound the flank steak until evenly thin. Spread the basil pesto over one steak, within 1 inch of the edge. Sprinkle with the sun-dried tomatoes. Sprinkle with 1½ cups mozzarella cheese and the Parmesan cheese. Top with the second piece of flank steak and carefully transfer to the slow cooker. Top with the marinara sauce.

3. Cover and cook on Low for 5 to 7 hours.

4. Sprinkle with the remaining cup of mozzarella cheese. Carefully remove the meat from the slow cooker and slice into servings.

PER SERVING: 633 CALORIES ★ FAT 39 G (55%) ★ NET CARBS 13 G (8%) ★ PROTEIN 49 G (31%)

Chipotle Beef with Fresh Tomato Salsa

SERVES
8

This Tex-Mex–flavored roast is so versatile. You can serve it on its own or topped with cheese, or fill lettuce leaves with the beef and salsa for a low-carb take on taco night.

SLOW COOKER SIZE: MEDIUM

1 medium onion, chopped

2 tablespoons avocado oil

1 boneless beef chuck roast (2½ to 3 pounds), quartered

2 chipotle chiles in adobo sauce, chopped (see Tip, page 98)

2 teaspoons minced garlic

1 teaspoon chili powder

Salt and pepper

1 (14.5-ounce) can fire-roasted diced tomatoes, not drained

¼ cup beef broth or water

SALSA AND TOPPINGS

3 ripe tomatoes, chopped

1 jalapeño pepper, chopped

2 tablespoons minced cilantro

2 tablespoons fresh lime juice

1½ cups shredded cheddar cheese

1 cup full-fat sour cream

1 cup guacamole

1. Place the chopped onion in the slow cooker.

2. Heat the avocado oil in a large skillet over medium-high heat. Add the roast and brown well on each side, 8 to 10 minutes. Place the meat in the slow cooker on top of the onion. Spoon the chipotle chiles over the beef and spread to cover evenly. Season with the garlic, chili powder, salt, and pepper. Pour the tomatoes and broth over all.

3. Cover and cook on Low for 6 to 8 hours. Remove the roast. Using the tines of two forks, shred the meat. Return the meat to the liquid.

4. In a medium bowl, stir together the tomatoes, jalapeño, cilantro, and lime juice. Season to taste with salt. Top each serving of beef with the salsa, cheddar cheese, sour cream, and guacamole.

PER SERVING: 589 CALORIES ★ FAT 45 G (69%) ★ NET CARBS 6 G (4%) ★ PROTEIN 35 G (24%)

Beef Stroganoff

This classic dish is named after a nineteenth-century Russian diplomat, Count Paul Stroganov. On a keto diet, it is especially tasty served over zucchini noodles or Cauliflower Mash (page 64).

SERVES 8

SLOW COOKER SIZE: MEDIUM

3 tablespoons olive oil

1 boneless beef chuck roast (about 2 pounds), cut into cubes

½ teaspoon salt

½ teaspoon ground black pepper

1 medium onion, chopped

4 garlic cloves, minced

2 cups sliced white button mushrooms

1 cup beef broth

2 tablespoons arrowroot powder

1 cup full-fat sour cream

1. Rub the sides and bottom of the stoneware with 1 tablespoon of the olive oil.

2. Heat the remaining 2 tablespoons olive oil in a large skillet over medium-high heat. Add the beef and season with salt and pepper. Brown the beef on all sides, 4 to 6 minutes. Place in the slow cooker. Add the onion, garlic, and mushrooms and stir to combine. Pour in the broth.

3. Cover and cook on Low for 6 to 8 hours. Remove about ½ cup liquid from the slow cooker and whisk in the arrowroot. Return the arrowroot mixture to the slow cooker and whisk to combine. Cover and cook on High for about 10 to 15 minutes to allow mixture to thicken.

4. Whisk in the sour cream. Serve warm.

PER SERVING: 398 CALORIES ★ FAT 31 G (70%) ★ NET CARBS 4 G (4%) ★ PROTEIN 24 G (24%)

★ TIP: Many people say that classic Korean chili flakes, also known as gochurgaru, are essential for spicy Korean dishes. These flakes do not contain the chili seeds, so they are milder than common red pepper flakes. Korean chile flakes are readily available at Asian markets and on-line, and they come in different degrees of heat. If you don't have them on hand, substitute with chili powder and a pinch of red pepper flakes.

Korean-Style Short Ribs

Korean ribs are known for their spicy flavor. The sauce features Asian pear, which adds flavor and replaces the sugar, keeping the net carbs quite low.

SERVES
8

4 pounds beef short ribs, English cut (cut between the bones), in 2- to 3-inch lengths (see Tip)

1 cup cubed peeled Daikon radish

1 tablespoon dried minced garlic

1½ tablespoons Korean chile flakes or chili powder (see Tip, opposite)

Salt and ground black pepper

1 medium onion, cut into wedges

1 (2-inch) piece fresh ginger, thinly sliced

1 Asian pear, peeled, cored, and cubed

¼ cup rice vinegar

2 tablespoons soy sauce

2 tablespoons sesame oil

1. Place the ribs in a large bowl and cover with cold water. Allow the ribs to soak for 30 minutes to remove any blood or residue. Drain the ribs, rinse, and pat dry.

2. Place the radish in the slow cooker. Place the ribs in the slow cooker. Season the ribs with the garlic, chile flakes, salt, and pepper.

3. In the work bowl of a food processor, combine the onion, ginger, and pear. Pulse until finely chopped. Add the vinegar and process until almost a smooth puree. Spoon the onion–vinegar mixture over the ribs. Drizzle with the soy sauce and sesame oil.

4. Cover and cook on Low for 7 to 9 hours, or until the meat is tender.

★ TIP: Korean ribs are often cut in what is called a flaken cut, which means that the ribs are cut thinly across the bone. This thinner cut is typically used for Korean ribs, as they are prepared for a grill. For the English cut, specified in this recipe, the ribs are cut between the ribs. If you use the flaken cut for this recipe, decrease the cooking time to 4 to 6 hours, or until the meat is tender. Ask the butcher to help you and have them cut as you prefer.

PER SERVING: 934 CALORIES ★ FAT 86 G (83%) ★ NET CARBS 3 G (1%) ★ PROTEIN 34 G (15%)

Chicago Beef

Chicago is famous for its beef studded with pepperoncini peppers. This iconic recipe slow-cooks to perfection.

SERVES 6

SLOW COOKER SIZE: MEDIUM

3 tablespoons canola oil

1 boneless beef chuck roast (about 2 pounds)

1 teaspoon dried minced garlic

1 tablespoon dried Italian seasoning

½ cup jarred pepperoncini peppers, with liquid

1 cup beef broth

1. Rub the sides and bottom of the stoneware with 1 tablespoon of the canola oil.

2. Heat the remaining 2 tablespoons of canola oil in a large skillet over medium-high heat. Add the roast and brown well on each side, 8 to 10 minutes. Place the meat in the slow cooker. Sprinkle with the garlic and Italian seasonings. Sprinkle the peppers over all. Pour the beef broth over all.

3. Cover and cook on Low for 6 to 8 hours, or until the meat is tender. Remove the roast. Using the tines of two forks, shred the meat. Return the meat to slow cooker and serve with collected juices.

PER SERVING: 436 CALORIES ★ FAT 34 G (70%) ★ NET CARBS 1 G (1%) ★ PROTEIN 30 G (27%)

Rustic Short Rib Ragout

This rich, flavorful stew will rival any you might order at an Italian restaurant. The ribs are so tender, the meat falls off the bone.

SERVES
8

SLOW COOKER SIZE: LARGE

1 celery stalk, chopped

1 medium onion, chopped

6 slices sugar-free bacon

4 pounds beef short ribs, English cut (cut between the bones), about 2- to 3-inch lengths

¾ cup beef broth

2 teaspoons dried minced garlic

2 teaspoons dried Italian seasoning

2 bay leaves

1 (14.5-ounce) can diced tomatoes, not drained

½ cup dry red wine

½ cup shredded Parmesan cheese

2 tablespoons minced fresh basil

1. Place the celery and onion in the slow cooker.

2. In a large skillet over medium-high heat, cook the bacon until crisp, 6 to 10 minutes. Set the bacon aside. Add about half the ribs to the skillet and cook until browned, turning to brown evenly, 8 to 10 minutes. Transfer the browned ribs to the slow cooker. Repeat with the remaining ribs. Crumble the bacon and sprinkle it over the ribs.

3. Pour the broth into the skillet. Cook over medium-high heat, scraping up any browned bits of meat, until it boils. Cook, uncovered, for 2 to 3 minutes more. Pour the broth into the slow cooker.

4. Season the ribs with the garlic, Italian seasoning, and bay leaf. Pour the tomatoes and wine over the ribs. Cover and cook on Low for 7 to 9 hours, or until the meat is very tender.

5. Remove the ribs, both meat and bones. (Be sure to remove all the bones.) Discard the bay leaves. Carefully, use an immersion blender to puree the sauce until nearly smooth (see Tip, page 47). Shred the meat and discard the bones. Return the meat to the sauce and stir to blend. Cover and cook on High for 15 to 30 minutes. Before serving, sprinkle with Parmesan cheese and fresh basil.

PER SERVING: 1,004 CALORIES ★ FAT 91 G (82%) ★ NET CARBS 3 G (1%) ★ PROTEIN 38 G (15%)

Braised Brisket with Onions

This hearty dish is perfect for any family dinner. The slow cooker does all the work and braises the meat on low heat, making it flavorful and tender.

SERVES

10

SLOW COOKER SIZE: LARGE

3 tablespoons olive oil

2 medium onions, sliced

1 beef brisket (about 4 pounds), cut in half

1½ teaspoons kosher salt

½ teaspoon ground black pepper

1 teaspoon dried minced garlic

2 celery stalks, sliced

1 bay leaf

1 teaspoon dried thyme

1 (14.5-ounce) can diced tomatoes, not drained

½ cup dry red wine

1 cup beef broth

3 tablespoons minced fresh flat-leaf (Italian) parsley

1. Rub the sides and bottom of the stoneware with 1 tablespoon of the olive oil. Place the onions in the slow cooker.

2. Heat the remaining 2 tablespoons olive oil in a large skillet over medium-high heat. Add the brisket and brown well on each side, 8 to 10 minutes. Place the meat over the onions. Season with the salt, pepper, and garlic. Top with the celery, bay leaf, thyme, and tomatoes. Pour the wine and broth around the edges of the meat.

3. Cover and cook on Low for 6 to 8 hours, or until the meat is tender. Remove the meat from the slow cooker and place on a serving platter. Remove and discard the bay leaf. Use a slotted spoon to lift out the onions and vegetables, and place them on the brisket. Spoon the drippings over all. Sprinkle with the parsley. Cover and allow to stand for 10 minutes, then carve thinly across the grain.

PER SERVING: 577 CALORIES ★ FAT 44 G (69%) ★ NET CARBS 5 G (3%) ★ PROTEIN 34 G (23%)

CONDIMENTS, SAUCES, AND STOCKS

Caramelized Onions

This just might become your favorite ingredient for adding a pop of flavor to a dish. Use the caramelized onions to top a steak, chop, roast, or burger. Make a batch, then divide into freezer containers, label, and freeze them for future use.

SERVES

16

SLOW COOKER SIZE: LARGE

2 tablespoons olive oil

6 sweet yellow onions, thinly sliced

4 tablespoons butter

Salt and pepper

1. Rub the sides and bottom of the stoneware with the olive oil. Place the onions in the slow cooker. Dot with the butter.

2. Cover and cook on High for 5 to 7 hours, or until the onions are caramelized. Season to taste with salt and pepper.

PER (1/4 CUP) SERVING: 57 CALORIES ★ FAT 5 G (78%) ★ NET CARBS 3 G (21%) ★ PROTEIN 0G 0%)

Bolognese Sauce

Bolognese sauce, otherwise known as ragout, is traditionally cooked slowly all day, so it is a perfect match for the slow cooker. Place the ingredients in the pot and have a great meat sauce by dinnertime.

SERVES

8

SLOW COOKER SIZE: LARGE

3 tablespoons olive oil

1 medium onion, chopped

1 pound Italian sausage

1 pound ground beef

4 garlic cloves, minced

2 (28-ounce) cans crushed tomatoes

2 tablespoon dried basil

1 tablespoon minced fresh oregano

1 cup beef broth

½ teaspoon salt

1. Rub the sides and bottom of the stoneware with 1 tablespoon of the olive oil.

2. Heat 1 tablespoon of the olive oil in a large skillet over medium-high heat. Add the onion and cook until tender, stirring frequently, 3 to 5 minutes. Place in the slow cooker.

3. Heat the remaining tablespoon olive oil in the skillet. Add the sausage and ground beef and cook until browned, stirring to crumble as you cook, 8 to 10 minutes. Pour the cooked meats into the slow cooker along with the remaining ingredients.

4. Cover and cook on Low for 6 to 8 hours.

PER SERVING: 514 CALORIES ★ FAT 40 G (70%) ★ NET CARBS 12 G (9%) ★ PROTEIN 20 G (16%)

Queso

Ladle this luscious cheese sauce over any grilled meat, serve it as dip with cauliflower, or create a Tex-Mex bowl with seasoned meat, grilled peppers, and queso, topped with guacamole.

SERVES 14

SLOW COOKER SIZE: SMALL

1 tablespoon avocado oil

2 tablespoons butter

½ medium onion, chopped

2 garlic cloves, minced

1 (14.5-ounce) can petite diced tomatoes, not drained

½ cup chopped jarred roasted green chiles (see Tip)

16 ounces shredded sharp cheddar cheese (2 cups)

½ cup chicken broth

½ cup heavy whipping cream

1. Rub the sides and bottom of the stoneware with the avocado oil.

2. Melt the butter in a medium skillet over medium-high heat. Add the onion and cook or until tender, stirring frequently, 3 to 5 minutes. Stir in the garlic and cook for 30 seconds more. Transfer the onion to the slow cooker. Stir in the tomatoes, chiles, cheese, and broth.

3. Cover and cook on High for 1 hour, or until melted, stirring every 15 minutes.

4. Stir in the cream. Cover and cook on High for 15 minutes. Turn down to Low for serving.

★ TIP: You can use any kind of roasted chiles you enjoy. Hatch chiles, a popular New Mexico variety, are now available in jars, as are a variety of other canned roasted chiles. For a milder queso, substitute 2 (4-ounce) cans of whole green chiles, drained and chopped. Or, if you wish, use fresh chiles. To roast fresh chiles, cut them in half and remove the stem and seeds. Place them flat, skin side up, on a baking sheet. Spray with nonstick cooking spray, then broil 10 to 15 minutes, or until charred and dark brown. Place the chiles in a bowl and cover with a cloth; allow to stand 10 to 15 minutes, then peel and chop.

PER (1/4 CUP) SERVING: 200 CALORIES ★ FAT 17 G (76%) ★ NET CARBS 3 G (6%) ★ PROTEIN 7 G (14%)

Marinara Sauce

Typically, marinara sauce simmers all day and requires frequent stirring. This is where the slow cooker saves the day. Add all the ingredients and slow-cook, with no stirring or fuss.

SERVES

12

SLOW COOKER SIZE: LARGE

4 tablespoons olive oil

1 cup chopped onion

8 garlic cloves, minced

1 cup beef broth

¼ cup minced fresh parsley

1 tablespoon dried basil

2 teaspoons dried oregano

½ teaspoon salt

½ teaspoon ground black pepper

2 bay leaves

1 can (28-ounce) crushed tomatoes

1 can (28-ounce) tomato puree

1 can (6-ounce) tomato paste

1. Rub the sides and bottom of the stoneware with 1 tablespoon of the olive oil.

2. Heat the remaining 3 tablespoons olive oil in a large skillet over medium-high heat.

3. Add the onion and cook until tender, stirring frequently, 3 to 5 minutes. Add the garlic and cook for 1 minute more. Spoon the onion and garlic into the slow cooker. Add the remaining ingredients to the slow cooker, and stir to blend well.

4. Cover and cook on Low for 7 to 9 hours.

5. Remove and discard the bay leaves just before serving.

PER SERVING: 104 CALORIES ★ FAT 5 G (43%) ★ NET CARBS 10 G (38%) ★ PROTEIN 3 G (11%)

Barbecue Sauce

There are perhaps as many recipes for barbecue sauce as there are people who enjoy barbecue. This recipe makes a richly flavored tomato-based sauce that tastes just a little sweet and spicy. To use the sauce, brush it over smoked or grilled meat toward the end of the cooking period. Or, serve it as a warm dip with pieces of grilled steak, sausages, or ribs.

SERVES

16

SLOW COOKER SIZE: SMALL

2 tablespoons avocado oil

8 tablespoons butter

1 (14.5-ounce) can petite diced tomatoes, not drained

2 (6-ounce) cans tomato paste

⅔ cup apple cider vinegar

1½ tablespoons granulated erythritol sweetener

4 teaspoons chili powder

4 teaspoons smoked paprika (see Tip, page 102)

4 teaspoons mustard powder

1 tablespoon dried minced garlic

1 teaspoon salt

1 teaspoon celery seeds

1 teaspoon onion powder

½ teaspoon ground black pepper

¼ teaspoon hot sauce

½ cup chicken broth

1. Rub the sides and bottom of the stoneware with the avocado oil.

2. Place the butter in the slow cooker. Add the remaining ingredients and stir to blend. Cover and cook on Low for 2½ to 3½ hours.

3. Carefully, use an immersion blender to puree the mixture until nearly smooth (see Tip, page 47).

PER (1/4 CUP) SERVING: 99 CALORIES ★ FAT: 8 G (73%) ★ NET CARBS 6 G (24%) ★ PROTEIN 2 G (8%)

Chicken Bone Stock

No need to buy commercially prepared stock when it is this easy, and flavorful, to prepare at home. Use the stock in your favorite recipe or ladle 1- or 2-cup portions into freezer containers, then label, date, and freeze. When you're ready to use, thaw and add to the recipe you are making.

MAKES ABOUT 7 CUPS

SLOW COOKER SIZE: LARGE

2 to 3 pounds bone-in chicken pieces, especially bony pieces such as wings and backs

1 medium onion, quartered

2 celery stalks, leaves removed, cut into 2-inch pieces

4 or 5 whole black peppercorns, or ½ teaspoon ground black pepper

½ teaspoon kosher salt

2 sprigs fresh Italian (flat-leaf) parsley, about 2 inches long

2 sprigs fresh thyme, about 2 inches long

6 cups water

1. Place all the ingredients in the slow cooker. Cover and cook on Low for 8 to 10 hours.

2. Allow the stock to cool slightly. Place a fine-mesh strainer over a deep bowl. Carefully ladle the stock into the strainer. Discard the meat, bones and vegetables.

★ TIP: Often in everyday cooking, the terms "broth" and "stock" are used interchangeably, but technically there is a difference. Currently, "bone broth" is popular and by food definitions, bone broth is actually stock. Confusing? Yes, but no worries. Both broth and stock begin by cooking meat or chicken in water. Stock is made by cooking the bones for a long time, so it has a richer mouthfeel from the gelatin in the bones. Broth may or may not have been made from bones, but it begins by cooking a meat. Stock is used as an ingredient in other dishes, so it is left unseasoned—or at most, is very mildly seasoned—but broth is seasoned so you can serve it as a light soup. However, they are very similar, and for the recipes in this book you may substitute stock, especially your own homemade stock, for the broth listed in the recipe.

PER CUP: 423 CALORIES ★ FAT 37 G (79%) ★ NET CARBS 1 G (1%) ★ PROTEIN 19 G (18%)

Beef Bone Stock

A rich beef stock is one of the building blocks of great-tasting dishes. It is so easy to prepare, and the flavor is unbeatable. Use the stock in your favorite recipe, or ladle 1- or 2-cup portions into freezer containers, then label, date, and freeze. When you're ready to use, thaw and add to the recipe you are making.

MAKES ABOUT 7 CUPS

SLOW COOKER SIZE: LARGE

4 tablespoons avocado oil

2 to 3 pounds meaty beef bones, such as oxtails, beef shanks, or marrow bones

1 medium onion, quartered

2 celery stalks, leaves removed, quartered

3 garlic cloves, halved

1 bay leaf

½ teaspoon dried thyme

½ teaspoon kosher salt

6 to 8 black peppercorns

1 tablespoon apple cider vinegar

6 cups water

1. Heat 2 tablespoons of the avocado oil in a large skillet over medium-high heat. Add about half of the meat and brown well on each side, 8 to 10 minutes. Place the browned meat in the slow cooker. Add the remaining 2 tablespoons oil to the skillet, brown the rest of the meat, and place it in the slow cooker. Add the remaining ingredients.

2. Cover and cook on Low for 10 to 12 hours.

3. Allow the stock to cool slightly. Place a fine-mesh strainer over a deep bowl. Carefully ladle the stock into the strainer. Discard the meat, bones, and vegetables.

> ★ TIP: If you want to freeze the stock in smaller portions, get out your muffin pans. Many times, a muffin pan will hold ⅓ to ½ cup stock in each of the cups. Ladle the stock into the cups and freeze. Once firm, remove the cubes of stock from the muffin pan and seal them in a freezer bag. Be sure to label and date the bag. Whenever you need a small amount of stock, just add the frozen cube to the soup, stew, or dish. For optimum flavor, plan to use frozen stock in 1 to 2 months.

PER CUP: 355 CALORIES ★ FAT 24 G (61%) ★ NET CARBS 2 G (2%) ★ PROTEIN 32 G (36%)

DESSERTS

Lemon Cake with Buttercream Frosting

Lemon is a delightful, fresh flavor for dessert. Bake this cake and share it with your friends over coffee, serve it after brunch, or let it take center stage on the dessert buffet. It will be a hit any time and at any event.

SERVES
8

SLOW COOKER SIZE: LARGE

CAKE

Nonstick cooking spray

1¾ cups almond flour

½ teaspoon baking powder

¼ teaspoon baking soda

¼ teaspoon salt

¼ teaspoon xanthan gum

Zest of 1 lemon

8 tablespoons unsalted butter, softened

4 ounces full-fat cream cheese, softened

⅔ cup granulated erythritol sweetener

3 large eggs

1 tablespoon fresh lemon juice

1 teaspoon lemon extract

1. Line a 7-inch springform pan with parchment paper. Spray with nonstick cooking spray. Place a rack about 1 inch high in the slow cooker.

2. In a medium bowl, whisk together the almond flour, baking powder, baking soda, salt, xanthan gum, and lemon zest. Set aside.

3. In a large bowl, using a handheld mixer at medium-high speed, beat together the butter and cream cheese for 1 minute. Beat in sweetener. Add the eggs, one at a time, beating well after each addition. Beat in the lemon juice and lemon extract. On low speed, beat in the almond flour mixture, mixing just until blended. Spoon into the prepared pan. Cover the pan with aluminum foil.

4. Place the filled pan on the rack in the slow cooker. Cover and cook on High for 2½ to 3½ hours, or until a wooden pick inserted into the center of the cake comes out clean.

PER SERVING (WITH FROSTING): 331 CALORIES ★ FAT 32 G (87%) ★ NET CARBS 33 G (40%) ★ PROTEIN 9 G (11%)

PER SERVING (WITHOUT FROSTING): 318 CALORIES ★ FAT 30 G (85%) ★ NET CARBS 18 G (23%) ★ PROTEIN 9 G (11%)

BUTTERCREAM FROSTING

1 tablespoon unsalted butter, melted

½ cup confectioners' erythritol sweetener

3 to 4 teaspoons fresh lemon juice

3 thin lemon slices, twisted (optional)

Mint leaves

5. Remove the pan from the slow cooker and place on a wire rack to cool for 15 minutes. Run a knife around the edges of the pan and remove the sides of the pan. Allow to cool completely.

6. Make the frosting: In a medium bowl, combine the melted butter, sweetener, and 3 teaspoons of the lemon juice. Stir until smooth and blended. Stir in the remaining 1 teaspoon lemon juice if a thinner frosting is desired. Spread the frosting over the cooled cake. If desired, garnish with thin lemon slices, twisted, and mint leaves.

Gingerbread with Maple Frosting

The classic spices of ginger, cinnamon, cloves, and nutmeg create a warm and comforting flavor and aroma. This is the perfect cake to bake for holiday gatherings.

SERVES 8

SLOW COOKER SIZE: LARGE

GINGERBREAD

Nonstick cooking spray

1¼ cups almond flour

1 tablespoon unsweetened cocoa powder

1 teaspoon baking powder

¼ teaspoon baking soda

¼ teaspoon salt

1½ teaspoons ground ginger

1 teaspoon ground cinnamon

¼ teaspoon ground cloves

¼ teaspoon ground nutmeg

10 tablespoons unsalted butter, softened

⅔ cup brown sugar erythritol sweetener, packed

3 large eggs

¼ cup cold brewed coffee

1. Line a 7-inch springform pan with parchment paper. Spray the pan with nonstick cooking spray. Place a rack about 1 inch high in the slow cooker.

2. In a small bowl, whisk together the flour, cocoa, baking powder, baking soda, salt, ginger, cinnamon, cloves, and nutmeg. Set aside.

3. In a large bowl, using a handheld mixer at medium-high speed, beat together the butter and sweetener for 1 minute, or until creamy. Beat in the eggs, one at a time, beating well after each addition. Beat in the cold coffee. On low speed, mix in the almond flour mixture, blending just until moistened. Spoon into the prepared pan. Cover the pan with aluminum foil.

4. Place the filled pan on the rack in the slow cooker. Cover and cook on High for 2½ to 3½ hours, or until a wooden pick inserted in the center comes out clean.

RECIPE CONTINUES...

PER SERVING (WITH FROSTING): 342 CALORIES ★ FAT 34 G (89%) ★ NET CARBS 29 G (34%) ★ PROTEIN 7 G (8%)

PER SERVING (WITHOUT FROSTING): 259 CALORIES ★ FAT 25 G (87%) ★ NET CARBS 17 G (26%) ★ PROTEIN 6 G (9%)

MAPLE FROSTING

2 ounces full-fat cream cheese, softened

2 tablespoons unsalted butter, softened

½ cup confectioners' erythritol sweetener

1½ to 2 tablespoons heavy whipping cream

½ teaspoon maple extract

¼ cup chopped pecans, toasted (see Tip, page 70)

5. Remove the pan from the slow cooker and place on a wire rack to cool for 15 minutes. Run a knife around the edges of the pan and remove the sides of the pan. Allow to cool completely.

6. Make the frosting: In a medium bowl, using a handheld mixer at medium speed, beat together the cream cheese and butter until creamy. Beat in the confectioners' sweetener. Beat in 1½ tablespoons of the cream. If a thinner frosting is desired, beat in the remaining cream. Beat in the maple extract. Frost the top of the cake. Sprinkle with the toasted pecans.

Classic Cheesecake

The slow cooker is known for producing slow, even, moist heat—just exactly the environment needed to bake a great cheesecake.

SERVES
8

SLOW COOKER SIZE: LARGE

CRUST

Nonstick cooking spray

½ cup sliced almonds, toasted (see Tip, page 70)

¼ cup almond flour

2 tablespoons unsalted butter, melted

½ teaspoon granulated erythritol sweetener

FILLING

2 (8-ounce) packages full-fat cream cheese, softened

¼ cup granulated erythritol sweetener

2 large eggs

2 tablespoons almond flour

3 tablespoons heavy whipping cream

1 teaspoon pure vanilla extract

½ teaspoon almond extract

¼ cup sliced almonds, toasted (see Tip, page 70)

½ cup fresh raspberries

Mint leaves

1. Make the crust: Preheat the oven to 375°F. Line a 7-inch springform pan with parchment. Spray with nonstick cooking spray. Place a rack about 1 inch high in the slow cooker.

2. In the work bowl of a food processor, combine the almonds, almond flour, melted butter, and sweetener. Pulse until the mixture resembles coarse meal. Add it to the prepared pan, and press to cover the bottom evenly. Bake until golden, 5 to 6 minutes. Set aside to cool completely.

3. Make the filling: In a large bowl, using a hand-held mixer at medium-high speed, beat the cream cheese until creamy. Beat in the sweetener. Add the eggs, one at a time, beating well. Beat in the flour, cream, vanilla, and almond extract. Pour into the crust. Cover the pan with foil, and place on the rack in the slow cooker. Cover and cook on High for 2½ to 3½ hours, until the cheesecake is softly set.

4. Turn the slow cooker off and let the cheesecake cool in the covered slow cooker for 1 hour. Remove the cheesecake and cool to room temperature. Refrigerate for 4 hours, or up to overnight.

5. Run a knife around the edges of the pan and remove the sides. Just before serving, garnish the cheesecake with almonds, raspberries, and mint. Store leftovers in the refrigerator.

PER SERVING: 342 CALORIES ★ FAT 33 G (87%) ★ NET CARBS 12 G (14%) ★ PROTEIN 8 G (9%)

Berry Cobbler

Juicy, warm berries nestled in a buttery crust is the dessert dreams are made of. And just when it couldn't get any better, sweetened whipped cream tops it all off.

SERVES 6

SLOW COOKER SIZE: MEDIUM

FILLING

2 tablespoons unsalted butter, softened

2 (16-ounce) packages frozen, no-sugar added mixed berries

4 teaspoons granulated erythritol sweetener

¼ teaspoon xanthan gum

CRUST

1 cup almond flour

¼ teaspoon baking powder

¼ teaspoon ground nutmeg

Dash salt

4 tablespoons unsalted butter, melted

¼ cup granulated erythritol sweetener

2 large eggs

1 teaspoon pure vanilla extract

¼ cup sliced almonds, toasted (see Tip, page 70)

WHIPPED CREAM

1 cup heavy whipping cream

2 tablespoons confectioners' erythritol sweetener

1. Make the filling: Rub the sides and bottom of the stoneware with the butter. Pour in the frozen berries and the sweetener. Cover and cook on High for 2 hours. Stir in the xanthan gum.

2. Make the crust: In a small bowl, whisk together the almond flour, baking powder, nutmeg, and salt. Set aside.

3. In a medium bowl, whisk together the butter and sweetener. Whisk in the eggs and vanilla. Whisk the dry ingredients into the butter mixture. Dollop the crust over the hot berries.

4. Cover and cook on High for 1 to 1½ hours, or until the crust is set. Sprinkle with the almonds.

5. Turn the slow cooker off. Allow to stand, covered, for 30 minutes. Spoon into serving bowls.

6. Make the whipped cream: In a deep bowl, using a handheld mixer at medium speed, beat the cream until frothy. Gradually beat in the sweetener. Increase the speed to high and beat until stiff peaks form. Dollop the whipped cream onto each serving.

PER SERVING: 468 CALORIES ★ FAT 40 G (77%) ★ NET CARBS 34 G (29%) ★ PROTEIN 9 G (8%)

INDEX

Also available everywhere books are sold:
THE ESSENTIAL VEGETARIAN KETO COOBOOK
THE ESSENTIAL VEGAN KETO COOKBOOK

RODALE